Information Systems Engineering Library

Applying Soft Systems Methodology to an SSADM Feasibility Study

CCTA

November 1993

LONDON: HMSO

For further information regarding this
publication and other CCTA products please
contact:

CCTA Library
Riverwalk House
157-161 Millbank
London SW7P 4RT

071-217 3331

Contents

Foreword

The **Information Systems Engineering Library**
provides guidance on managing and carrying out
Information Systems Engineering activities. In the IS life
cycle, Information Systems Engineering takes place once
the IS strategy has been defined. It is concerned with
the development and ongoing improvement of
information systems up to the operational stage, when
systems become the responsibility of infrastructure
management.

The Information Systems Engineering Library builds on
guidance in the CCTA IS Guides, particularly set A:
Management and Planning Set and set B: *Systems
Development Set* and complements other CCTA
products, in particular the project management method,
PRINCE, and the systems analysis and design method,
SSADM.

Volumes in the Information Systems Engineering
Library are of interest to varying levels of staff from IS
directors to IS providers, helping them to improve the
quality and productivity of their IS development work.
Some volumes in this library should also be of interest
to business managers, IS users and those involved in
market testing, whose business operations depend on
having effective IS support by means of Information
Systems Engineering activities.

The Information Systems Engineering Library also
complements other related CCTA publications,
particularly the IT Infrastructure Library for operational
issues and the IS Planning Subject Guides for strategic
issues.

CCTA welcomes customer views on Information
Systems Engineering Library publications. Please send
your comments to:

Customer Services
Information Systems Engineering Group
Gildengate House
Upper Green Lane
NORWICH
NR3 1DW

Acknowledgements

The assistance of Brian Wilson, Lancaster University, Ulla Kingsley and John Hall, Model Systems Ltd, and Paul Turner, BIS, is gratefully acknowledged.

CCTA is pleased to acknowledge Professor Peter Checkland of the University of Lancaster as the originator of the Soft Systems Methodology. Extracts from his published works are used in this volume (see section 1.8).

In the glossary, the following definitions are copyright of John Wiley and Sons Ltd publishers of 'Systems Thinking, Systems Practice', 1981, by Peter Checkland. These definitions are reproduced with Wileys' kind permission: activity, actor, Catwoe, conceptual model, customer, environmental constraints, human activity system, model, owner, problem situation, rich picture, root definition, system, transformation process, Weltanschauung.

1 Introduction

1.1 Purpose

The purpose of this volume is to provide a general description of how to apply Soft Systems Methodology (SSM) to an SSADM feasibility study. The guidance aims to show how personnel involved in feasibility studies can use SSM concepts to define comprehensive business requirements so that systems developed using IS planning inputs and SSADM techniques more fully meet the real needs of the organisation.

SSM, itself a means for resolving problems, is used to extend the scope of feasibility study activities beyond those supported by SSADM. The SSM approach assists understanding of the many simultaneous views which may exist on what an organisation is trying to achieve. This allows potential interfaces to a system and factors affecting system implementation, including those unrelated to IS, to be investigated thoroughly.

SSM is particularly useful where business requirements are unclear, there are conflicting interests, or the proposed system is contentious. SSM also may be applied to good effect where changes in business processes or organisational structure are likely.

In combining the two approaches, the systematic method for developing systems provided by SSADM is preceded by an assessment of business needs. Better use is made of SSADM resources during the feasibility study and the time taken to conduct subsequent requirements analysis and specification can be reduced.

1.2 Relationship with other CCTA guidance on feasibility studies

IS Guide B2: *The Feasibility Study* gives a full account of what a feasibility study is, why it is needed and how it should be managed. Annex F of Guide B2 outlines SSADM Version 3 steps involved in Problem Definition.

SSADM Version 4 has a separate Feasibility Study Module in which core techniques are used to help identify IS requirements and determine whether proposed systems are technically feasible. The module notes SSM as being appropriate for business appraisal.

This volume describes the general concepts of SSM and how they can be applied to information systems before considering possible interfaces with SSADM.

| 1.3 | **Who should read this volume** | The volume is primarily intended for analysts involved in a feasibility study team who wish to use SSM in conjunction with SSADM. The guidance also may be useful to those with responsibility for the overall management of feasibility studies, users participating in such studies and to IS strategists. |

| 1.4 | **Assumed knowledge** | It is assumed that readers either understand or can make themselves familiar with the basic concepts and essential features of SSADM as these are not described in this volume. |

| 1.5 | **Structure of this volume** | Chapter 2 gives an overview of feasibility studies, describes the origins of SSM, and lists the advantages of applying SSM to a feasibility study. |

Chapter 3 describes the basic concepts of SSM and Chapter 4 describes in more detail the form SSM takes when it is applied to IS. Chapter 5 then shows how this form of SSM can interface with SSADM Feasibility Stage activities and individual SSADM products.

| 1.6 | **Terminology** | The volume follows conventions for SSADM and SSM terms used by reference books listed in the Bibliography and section 1.8 respectively. Thus 'Requirements Catalogue', an SSADM product, has initial capitals but not 'root definition', an SSM concept. |

| 1.7 | **How to use this volume** | The general description of how SSM might be applied to an SSADM feasibility study is not intended to be definitive. The approach needs to be tailored to the requirements of a particular feasibility study and of the particular organisation in which it is undertaken. Readers familiar with SSM concepts and the application of those concepts to IS may wish to omit Chapters 3 and 4 and proceed directly to Chapter 5. |

A feasibility study is a project in its own right and should be run under a formal project management method such as PRINCE, details of which may be found in the PRINCE set of guides. The Quality Guide of this set explains quality review procedures.

1.7.1 Competence in SSM

SSM provides an approach to solving management problems which requires skill and judgement. Readers are strongly recommended to attain or have attained a level of competence in SSM before attempting to apply it. Three levels of competence might be expected to be gained through appropriate training and practice:

- appreciation

- initial practitioner

- practitioner.

An appreciation of SSM may be gained by attending a formal training course. Such a course, lasting perhaps one day for senior management and two to three days for other staff, should:

- present the underlying theory

- provide practice in applying that theory

- depict its application to various situations.

A formal course to reach the level of initial practitioner should cover the same theoretical content as an appreciation course, but allow two to three days more for practical exercises.

Having assimilated the theory, experience in applying it is gained through practice along with appropriate coaching. Moving from initial practitioner to practitioner requires the ownership and commitment associated with a project. Guidance or assistance from an experienced practitioner is helpful here.

1.8   Reference material

The Soft Systems Methodology was developed through an action research programme at the University of Lancaster. The work is described in the following three texts:

- Checkland, P. B.
  Systems Thinking, Systems Practice
  John Wiley and Sons 1981
  ISBN 0 471 27911 0

- Wilson, B.
  Systems: Concepts, Methodologies and Applications
  John Wiley and Sons 1984
  ISBN 0 471 92716 3

- Checkland and Scholes
  Soft Systems Methodology in Action
  John Wiley and Sons 1990
  ISBN 0 471 92768 6

Details of other publications referred to in the text are given in the Bibliography.

2   Overview of feasibility studies and SSM

2.1   Feasibility study

A feasibility study should focus primarily on how and whether a proposed information system will help the organisation meet its business objectives. Issues involving the choice of implementation technology may require a more specialised type of study outside the scope of this publication. The aims of a feasibility study are to define an information system that will meet customer needs and provide flexibility for the future within the context of the organisation's IS strategy. The feasibility study should identify significant business and financial benefits which can be delivered by the system.

A feasibility study is normally initiated within the framework of an IS strategy and may result from an analysis of opportunities or problems perceived in a particular part of the organisation. The feasibility study defines initial user requirements and IS options and may be thought of as an intermediate study between IS strategy, based on analysis of an organisation or business, and application development, based on systems analysis. It builds on work produced during the strategy study to a level detailed enough for management to assess the implications of proceeding further.

2.1.1   Team composition

The feasibility study team should include staff who have a wide knowledge of how the business area under study operates, who understand the technical issues and who are able to relate business needs to Information Technology (IT) opportunities. Necessary skills include business analysis, systems analysis (especially SSADM) and project management. Management services and IS practitioners will have many of these skills. Ideally, an experienced SSM practitioner should join the team or provide support to its members to help them apply the methodology. The team may also require access to specialist advice including expertise in the strategic implications of choices of technical architecture.

2.1.2 Feasibility study scope

The feasibility study team members usually consider a number of information system options and recommend an option best fitted to meet the original requirements. They need to assess the desirability and feasibility of each option from the following considerations:

- support for business requirements and objectives now and in the future

- organisational and cultural acceptance

- viability of development and implementation route

- costs and benefits

- business, financial, technical, organisational and other risks.

The scope of IS includes both IT and non-IT based systems. Outputs from a feasibility study may include non-computer based information requirements which may suggest changes to parts of the organisation.

2.1.3 Feasibility Report

The major product of the feasibility study is the Feasibility Report. This contains an initial description of user requirements, describes IS and possibly other options, and documents management decisions about whether and how further work should proceed.

The report should be presented at the end of the study to those responsible for the monitoring, tuning and review functions of both IS strategy and tactical planning in addition to the commissioners of the study. From conclusions within the report, managers at the appropriate level need to decide whether to:

- commit resources to a further study

- proceed in a different direction from that first envisaged

- suspend the project

- cancel the project.

2.2   Origin of SSM

Many IS analysis methods assume systems can be engineered. They take the objective of a system as given and establish **how** it is to be achieved. Historically, this 'hard' approach failed when applied to less well-defined, or 'soft', situations faced by managers where trying to establish **what** is to be achieved is often the major part of the problem.

SSM evolved to address situations where there is no clear agreement on what the problem is. There may be different views and understandings of an organisation's main purpose and objectives which need to be considered to gain a full insight into the complete business area under study. Some of these views and understandings might be in conflict and accepted perceptions about an organisation may have to be questioned.

SSM can be adapted to suit a variety of situations and the range of analytical skills available to study them. It does not attempt to solve a specific type of problem but helps the analyst to understand a situation and suggest changes acceptable to management which might lead to improvements.

2.3   Applicability of SSM to a feasibility study

SSM provides a useful approach for ensuring that business needs are carried through from IS strategy to application development. Only those processes and information flows which will help satisfy business requirements are considered for inclusion in any proposed information system. Corporate policies and external constraints are taken into full account.

2.4   Advantages of SSM

SSM may be used to complement other approaches rather than replace them. The advantage of applying the methodology to a feasibility study is that it encourages the analyst to:

- concentrate on the business environment

- look at the area under study in the context of the whole organisation

- consider multiple perceptions and recognise that some may conflict

- analyse information required to monitor and control the operation of a proposed system should it be delivered

- communicate with users in their own terms.

2.4.1 Business environment

In SSM, the analyst forms definitions of what the business area is taken to be and its agreed tasks, ie its purpose, before defining what its information requirements are. SSM therefore:

- is driven from the context in which the information system is required

- is independent of any existing manual or automated procedures for processing information

- is well suited to deal with situations where there are no formal procedures for processing information

- caters for organisational changes since IS requirements are derived from a description of organisational tasks which is independent of any formal organisation structure.

SSM seeks to accommodate the concerns or needs of those who may be affected indirectly by a proposed information system as well as those likely to be affected directly.

2.4.2 Relevance to whole organisation

A study using SSM may recommend organisational restructuring, better-defined user roles, training requirements, and changes in business functions in addition to identifying information system requirements.

These issues may be addressed in SSADM when formulating Business System Options, but SSM provides a more formal means for separating the 'what', ie what changes are needed?, from the 'how', ie how can requirements be met using IS?

2.4.3 Multiple perceptions

Interested parties often have different perceptions as to the purpose of a business area. The skill in SSM is to select the most relevant set of perceptions, which often may be related to the accountability of individuals within the organisation. SSM is used to develop separate models of system activities to reflect those perceptions. The models are then combined in ways which seek to accommodate the various perceptions and may include extra activities to reconcile conflicting concerns or needs. Such combinations can help identify Business System Options and define acceptance criteria for the delivered system.

In SSADM requirements definition, there is provision for considering conflicting requirements in the creation of Business System Options and Technical System Options. However, there is no specific activity in the SSADM structural model that describes how to identify conflicts and reconcile them.

2.4.4 Monitor and control activities

SSM defines measures of performance for activities in a proposed system. Activities to monitor these measures and take control action to improve matters form an integral part of the proposed system.

2.4.5 Communication with users

The application of SSM leads to an assembly of arguments and a rationale that ought to be convincing to users. The soft systems approach provides the means for the analyst to discuss the situation in the users' own terms.

3   SSM: basic concepts

A number of approaches to problem solving have 'define the problem' as the first stage. This was also the starting point in the action research programme undertaken by the Systems Department at the University of Lancaster. A typical project in the early years of the programme was: To investigate ways of controlling the gas off-take temperature in a zinc smelter during transient operation. The problem is well defined and a solution is obtained when the temperature is controlled. This is a 'hard' problem. <u>How</u> to solve it is the concern. 'What is the problem?' is not a question to be answered; it is already stated.

It became apparent in later projects that situations were becoming more common in which the answer to the question: 'What is the problem?' was itself part of the problem. The definition of the problem was dependent upon who was asked and, since it was usually the case that more than one individual was concerned with the investigation, multiple definitions were frequently obtained. These were not always consistent and conflicting definitions were not uncommon. It is this dependency upon people and their perceptions that transform a problem from 'hard' to 'soft'.

The position of a problem within the spectrum from 'hard' to 'soft' is dependent upon the degree of diversity in the interpretations of the problems within a situation that can be said to be problematical by the individual in that situation. Observers of a flat tyre will all agree upon the nature of the problem but what to do to an economy to extract it from a recession is not characterised by such agreement.

The approach to problem solving which aims to explore such multiple interpretations of 'What is the problem' is called Soft Systems Methodology (SSM). This uses a specific concept; that of a human activity system (HAS), in which a particular interpretation of the word 'system' has been adopted.

3.1	'Hard' and 'Soft' approaches to problem solving

In taking a 'hard' view of a situation, the assumption is made that what constitutes a system is not problematic and that the system can be defined as a process or unit that exists in the real world. Thus a manufacturing unit, converting some raw material into a product, is represented by its physical boundary. It is generally assumed that the problem is one of 'engineering' the system by means of a systematic approach.

A 'soft' view takes the real world to be problematic and views 'the system' conceptually to facilitate the process of analysis. This is necessary in a 'soft' situation since the differing perceptions of people are an important variable that cannot be ignored. The manufacturing unit described above, for example, could be viewed as a system for achieving maximum utilisation of the production resources or, equally legitimately, as a system to satisfy a market demand.

The 'soft' approach to problem solving (SSM) is an organised way of reaching value judgements via a process of analysis that is explicit and defensible. A simple example may help to illustrate the form of SSM. Two people watching a television programme may, at the end of it, reach totally different conclusions about its quality. Although each will have observed the same screen display one may conclude that it was a good programme whereas the other may conclude that it was bad. There is little point in arguing which conclusion is right. They are probably both right but on the basis of totally different personal perceptions of what constitutes a good programme.

SSM consists of finding out about the situation which is the subject of investigation, making models relevant to perceptions pertaining to the situation and then reaching conclusions on the basis of a comparison of these models with the actual situation. To be completely defensible the models must be carefully constructed in a language appropriate to the nature of the real world. Thus the perceptions referred to in the above example can be made explicit so that they (not only the judgements made) can be scrutinised.

**3.2   Models of
purposeful activity**

However complex the real world may be, it can be assumed to be composed of people undertaking purposeful activity of various kinds. Individuals may not be pursuing activity with a consistent purpose relative to the other individuals, but they are not acting randomly. It is assumed that models of purposeful activity are useful constructs to help understand and hence explore the complexity of the real world.

In SSM, a systems model consists of a definition of what the system is, called a root definition, and a logically derived conceptual model, expressed as a linked set of purposeful activities, which describes what the system must do to be the one defined.

Each root definition represents a perception of the situation, <u>defined</u> as a particular Weltanschauung. Weltanschauung (W), a German word literally translated as 'world-view', is the set of assumptions or premises you believe to be true to support the view expressed. Since a particular situation in the real world is usually composed of a number of people with different perceptions, a number of conceptual models have to be constructed.

The number of models constructed does **not** equal the number of individuals. Each perception may contain a number of Ws with different emphases. Suppose that the situation of concern is the operation of prisons. Particular Ws may be expressed as:

- punishment

- rehabilitation

- security

- education.

A person is unlikely to perceive a prison to be 100% concerned with punishment or security or any other W, but will have a perception that is a mixture of some, or even all, the above Ws. Someone who operates a tough regime may be more oriented towards punishment than rehabilitation, whereas a more liberal-minded individual may emphasise education and rehabilitation rather than punishment. So although the number of individuals with a legitimate concern for a prison service (governors, chaplains, visitors) may be large, the number of Ws worth modelling can be quite small.

The analyst chooses to view the situation in a number of particular ways on the basis of significant Ws and, through the derivation of systems models and a comparison of them with the situation, assesses the implications of taking those views.

3.3 The transformation process

The basis for constructing a model of this kind is the assumption that at the core of purposeful activity is a transformation process (T), shown in Figure 1.

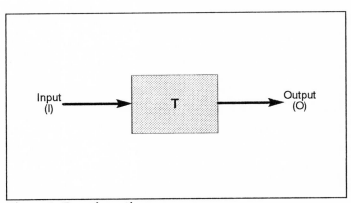

Figure 1: Transformation process

The real-world purposeful activity of a regional public housing directorate, could be: "to convert available housing within the jurisdiction of the directorate into housing occupied by the population of the region"

This is based on one W. There are other, equally valid, Ws, for example, bringing additional housing into the jurisdiction of the directorate or maximising return on investment.

3.4   Root definition

A root definition defines what a system is from a particular W. A root definition of a regional public housing directorate, constructed around the transformation process above, might be:

"A system, owned and operated by the Regional Housing Directorate, to provide housing for the population of the region to the benefit of both the region and the people, within the constraints of the locality, finance and relevant statutory regulations."

There are a number of elements that are common or represent identifiable characteristics within a root definition. These elements can be used to test if a root definition is well structured or well formulated rather than whether it is relevant or valid. They can be remembered by the mnemonic CATWOE in Table 1.

C	Customer	the recipient of the output of the transformation process
A	Actor	agents who would do the activities if the model were to map on to reality
T	Transformation	the process which transforms the system's input into its outputs. The transformation (T) may be expressed as the process itself or as an input converted into an output
W	Weltanschauung	world-view, the point of view or meaning attributed to the root definition
O	Owner	the wider system decision-taker with concern for the performance of the system
E	Environment	constraints, features of the real world that the definition needs to recognise but outside the control of the system's decision-taking process

Table 1: CATWOE elements

3.4.1 CATWOE analysis

Not all elements need be present. The elements that should be included to make a sensible root definition are the T and the W. The other elements are included or excluded on the judgment of the analyst with regard to their importance in relation to the particular study.

All CATWOE elements that are included in the root definition must be explicitly stated, with the exception of W which is always implicit. W is the answer to the question: "What must be believed for this definition to make sense?"

For the root definition given above, the CATWOE analysis is:

T   to provide housing for occupancy or, alternatively, available housing converted into occupied housing

C   the population of the region

A   the Regional Housing Directorate

O   the Regional Housing Directorate

E   constraints of the locality, finance and relevant statutory regulations

W   providing housing is beneficial to the region and to the people.

It is worth defining the T element first, since C is the recipient of the output and it is necessary to be clear about the output. Note that in this particular case, A and O are identical.

It should be re-stated that the root definition is the definition of an intellectual construct and not a description of the real world. Thus the analyst can choose who to take to be the owner, actor and customer in just the same way the analyst chooses what transformation, W and environmental constraints are worth modelling. They are all judgements but explicit judgements which may be changed as a result of the modelling and subsequent comparison.

3.4.2 Multiple perceptions

If there are a number of ways of perceiving a situation, which could be equally valid from the point of view of the people within the situation, then a number of root definitions should be formulated, each one representing a single W.

For instance, a past example of legislation which aroused feelings and resulted in conflicting views was the introduction of the Community Charge.

Suppose it had been required to implement a Community Charge within the jurisdiction of the Regional Housing Directorate. Relevant to this purposeful activity would have been the regional housing administrators, the particular government officers responsible for deriving the new policy and the members of the community who might have been expected to pay the charge. Successful implementation would have depended upon the perceptions and subsequent behaviour of all these individuals. Legitimate Ws of the Community Charge and its implementation might have been that it was a system to:

- produce a more equitable financial contribution to community services

- penalise households with multiple wage earners

- reward households with only one occupant

- increase the register of homeless

- increase the administrative burden of the Region's offices and their subsequent costs.

It is not argued that any of these would have been the correct description, only that evidence could have been collected from the individuals relevant to the purposeful activity which could have supported the claim to validity.

It might be argued, as in section 3.2, that none of these Ws were true in reality but that reality was a mixture of them all. It can also be argued that there was no mixture that could have been said to be correct. Each individual would have subscribed to a different emphasis within the mix. It might be the intention when implementing changes to minimise disadvantages implied in particular perceptions.

3.4.3 Primary task and issue-based root definitions

To cope with such complexity, the analyst has to decompose a mixture of multiple perceptions into a number of distinct single perceptions. It is usual to consider two types of root definition, those related to the primary task of an organisation and those related to issues within the situation.

The essential difference between these two types of definitions is that the primary task definition could be a description of the role of an organisation's administration, that is the boundary of the system could map on to the real-world organisation boundary and be coincident with it. An issue-based root definition is unlikely to be manifest as an organisational entity and would be expected to have a system boundary that had to map across organisation entities.

A primary task root definition relevant to the situation of a housing directorate might be: "A system to administer the financial and human resources available to the Housing Directorate for the benefit of the regional population."

An issue-based root definition could be: "A system to ensure collaboration between district administrators in the provision of services to the community."

Primary task root definitions are particularly useful in organisational restructuring and IS analysis. An issue-based analysis may well be relevant to the implementation of a computer-based information system and for strategic planning.

However, the application of SSM requires the flexible use of these concepts. Some variants of SSM may use only primary task analysis whereas others may use both primary task and issue-based definitions. SSM is not a technique but is a set of structured ways of using the concept of a human activity system; each structure being derived for the particular situation. The skilled analyst will construct a form of SSM to suit the nature of the situation under investigation.

Irrespective of whether the definition is primary task or issue-based, the derivation of the model which describes what the system must do is a logical process.

3.5 Conceptual model

A human activity system model, termed a 'conceptual model' to emphasise its status as an intellectual construct, can be derived from a root definition and defines what a system would have to do to be the system described in the root definition. It comprises the logically linked activities that would have to take place to satisfy the root definition. For example, Figure 2 is a conceptual model derived from root definition 1.

Root definition 1

"A system, owned and operated by the Regional Housing Directorate, to provide housing for the population of the region to the benefit of both the region and the people, within the constraints of the locality, finance and relevant statutory regulations."

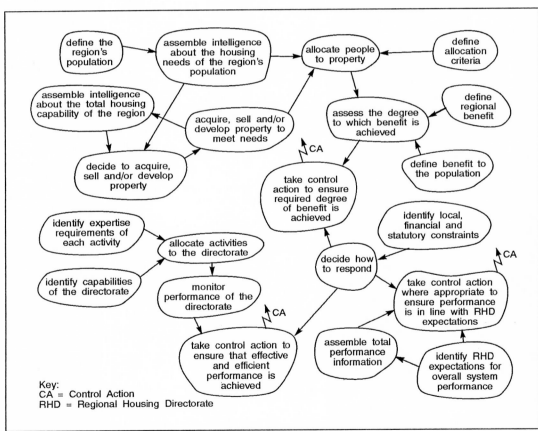

Figure 2: Conceptual model 1 derived from root definition 1

A conceptual model uses the language of verbs in the imperative to describe the purposeful activities making up the complete model.

Each individual purposeful activity is represented by an imperative verb phrase inside a boundary. Arrows represent logical dependencies; the activity at the head of an arrow cannot be carried out unless some information or resource is provided by the activity at the tail of the arrow. The crooked arrow indicates a temporary dependency according to where, ie to which activity, control action is directed.

3.5.1 Model construction

The conceptual model (CM), produced at the first level of resolution, is a direct answer to the question: "If the root definition (RD) states what the system is, what activities must it do, linked through which logical dependencies, in order to be that system?" This question must be answered with reference only to the words in the RD without recourse to the real world to which the system may be relevant. The processes of logic are all that are required. The structure of the RD needs to be analysed first (using CATWOE) in order to fully understand what the RD is saying. It is useful to then start the modelling process by representing the T. This is the major verb in the RD and defines the basic 'what'. The RD may also contain a constraint on the 'what' in terms of 'how' the system is to do it. Thus a 'system to do X by Y' is identifying that 'what' the system is doing is X and how it is doing it is through some mechanism Y. An alternative form may be 'a system to convert P into Q by doing Y'. Here the transformation is expressed as some input P converted into some output Q. Either form may be used.

An example will illustrate the process using some elements of CATWOE initially and introducing others as the process proceeds. It must be emphasised that although this example is completely general all RDs and all CMs need **not** be expressed in this way.

Let the initial root definition be:

"A system to do X by Y under the constraints E."

The model is illustrated in Figure 3. Although every activity in the model is under the constraints E, this may be included in the model by making each control activity logically dependent upon the decision of how to react, having first of all identified what they are. It may be noted that the 'how' of the transformation (Y) was modelled first and then its effect upon the achievement of X included.

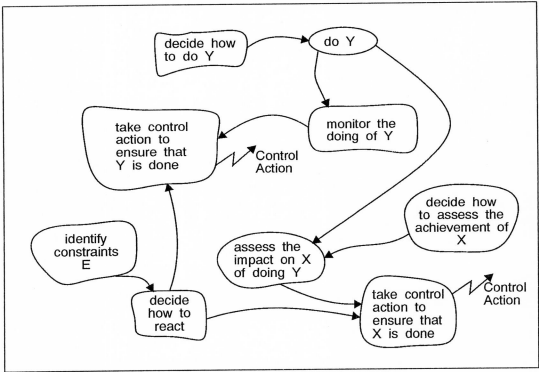

Figure 3: A system to do X by Y under the constraints E

Suppose the root definition is now:

"A system, owned by O, to do X by Y in order to achieve Z under the constraints E."

Since the owner (O) is the wider system decision taker the whole of the system must contribute to the achievement of the wider system's aims (ie be effective). Thus an overall control system must ensure that achieving Z through this mechanism is what the wider system needs. Hence the system must know what is expected of it and perform accordingly. The additional activities are illustrated in Figure 4.

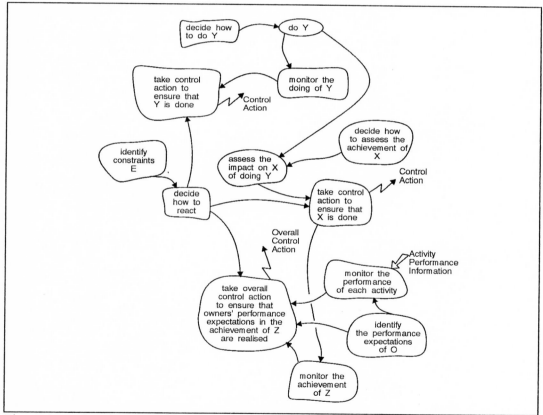

Figure 4: *A system owned by O to do X by Y in order to achieve Z under the constraints E*

Suppose that the root definition is now:

"A system, owned by O and operated with resources R, to do X by Y in order to achieve Z under the constraints E." The W contained in this RD is that "Z can be achieved by using the mechanism of doing X by Y." [If this belief is not held then the RD becomes meaningless].

The addition of 'actor' (ie resources R) means that the actor must be capable of doing all the activities; hence the matching of capabilities. C is the only element of CATWOE not now included but further elaboration of the model is unnecessary to demonstrate the process. The final developed model is illustrated in Figure 5.

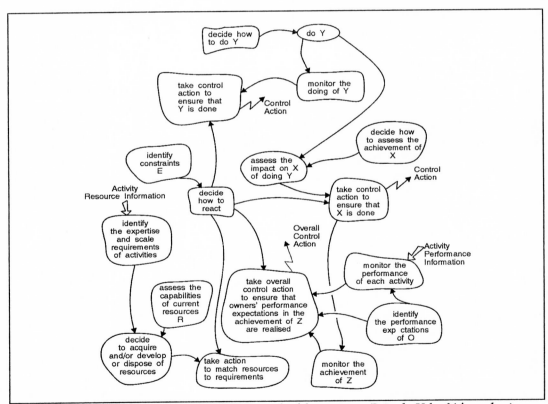

Figure 5:   A system owned by O and operated with resources R to do X by Y in order to achieve Z under the constraints E

All control systems are constrained as indicated by the presence of constraints E in the RD and hence so are all the activities. (They are all under the authority of the controllers). This model now represents the minimum necessary activities for the set of words in the RD. Logic only has been used as there is no actual real world that this model refers to because of its generality.

Although the form of root definition 1 is not identical with the general example here, the sets of activities relevant to the CATWOE elements have been identified in Figure 6.

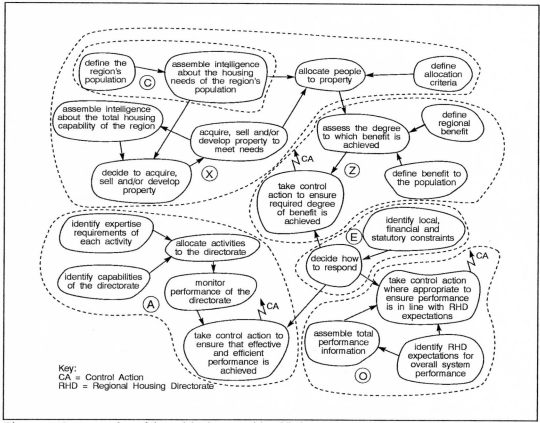

Figure 6: Conceptual model 1 with elements identified

The model in Figure 2 is not a description of the real-world activity of the Regional Housing Directorate. It would be equally legitimate to take a W of the situation which would lead to different activities within the model and different conclusions when compared with the actual situation. These models represent explicit ways of thinking about the problem situation and, because they are explicit, judgments based on their comparisons with the real world are defensible.

3.5.2 Model validation

Since they are models of particular Weltanschauungen (Ws) of the situation they cannot be validated in the same way that a simulation model of a production process could be. The reality that they are intended to explore is a complex mixture of a number of such Ws and, hence, each one is only partially relevant

They can, however, be validated as a model of a human activity system by comparing each one against the checklist given in Table 2.

objectives and purpose	Has the transformation T and any ways of doing it (hows) been properly represented?
connectivity	Are there any activities without sufficient logical dependencies?
measures of performance	Are expectations and resource capabilities represented through appropriate activities?
monitoring and control mechanism	Are the appropriate control systems specified? Are they dependent upon the proper monitoring activities? Are the spans of control identified by the phrases within the control activities?
decision-taking procedures	Are there any significant decisions (inferred from the RD) and have the necessary activities been included?
boundary	Is the scope of the activities in the model representative of, and no greater than, the span implied in the RD?
resources	Have any activities been included to match resources to the purpose of the system or will they emerge at higher resolution levels?
systems hierarchy	Has this been recognised through the inclusion of the owners expectations within a control system or was reference to O omitted from the RD? Is it useful to include subsystem boundaries around specific sets of activities?

Table 2: Checklist for validating conceptual model

Using the checklist should ensure that if omissions are made in developing the conceptual model, they are done so consciously. Satisfactory answers to the questions in the checklist will provide sufficient validation of the CM as a defensible model of a human activity system. Systems hierarchy is discussed in section 3.6.

3.6 Systems hierarchy

A conceptual model is a set of structured activities derived from a root definition. Each of these activities, or a set of them, can be taken as systems in their own right. For each such system, a root definition can be developed and a conceptual model derived from it. This process of expansion can be repeated to whatever level of detail is required.

This leads to the notion of a systems hierarchy in which a system can be expanded into subsystems and so on. Redefinition of a subsystem into a system means that the original system becomes a wider system. This, in turn, could be seen as a subsystem of a yet wider system. The root definition defines the location of a system within this hierarchy.

A systems hierarchy is illustrated in Figure 7. System 1 (defined by RD_1) can be taken to be an activity (or subsystem) within some wider system S_0. The wider system cannot be identified unless RD_1 specifies the owner of system 1. The conceptual model representing RD_1 describes what the system must do (as a set of activities) at resolution level 1.

Each activity, or group of activities, can be taken to be subsystems of S_1 and root definitions formulated to represent the CATWOE elements at this level. A consistent W must be maintained but the other elements of CATWOE will change to represent the increased level of detail. In the diagram, three subsystems, $SS_{1.1}$, $SS_{1.2}$ and $SS_{1.3}$, have been chosen yielding new root definitions, $RD_{1.1}$, $RD_{1.2}$ and $RD_{1.3}$. The identical process is now followed for each one yielding conceptual models corresponding to $S_{1.1}$, $S_{1.2}$ and $S_{1.3}$. This more detailed model is still the logical derivation of the original RD, ie S_1.

The systems hierarchy is represented by:

S_0 — Level 0

S_1 — Level 1

$S_{1.1}$, $S_{1.2}$, $S_{1.3}$ — Level 2

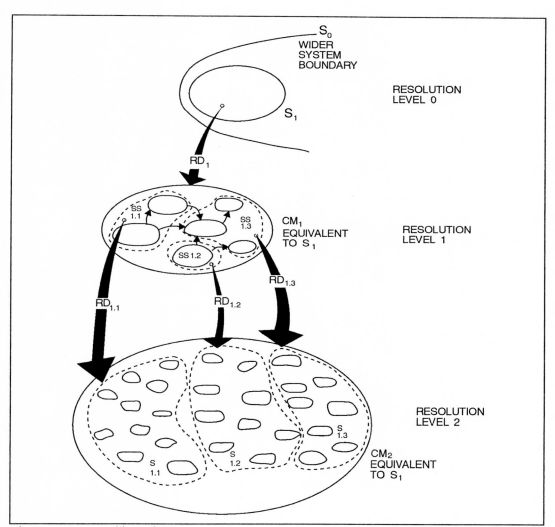

Figure 7: Systems hierarchy

For instance, in the housing example, a component W within the view of the regional estates officer might be represented by root definition 2 below:

Root definition 2

"A Regional Housing Directorate owned system to maximise the utilisation of its owned property in order to obtain a satisfactory return on its investment whilst recognising local, financial, statutory constraints and the regional housing policy."

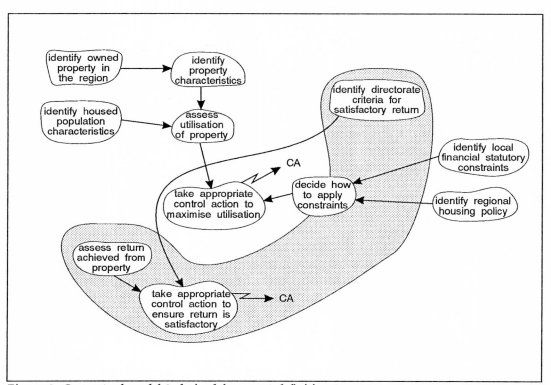

Figure 8: Conceptual model 2 derived from root definition 2

The shaded area in Figure 8 indicates a part of the conceptual model, dealing with return on investment, which is developed in more detail in Figure 9.

When a sub-model is developed in this way, it is
developed from a root definition such as root definition
2a:

Root definition 2a

"A Regional Accounts owned system which converts
the occupancy/non-occupancy of the region's property
into the revenue necessary to provide an adequate
return on investment while recognising statutory
constraints and the Region's policy with respect to
finance."

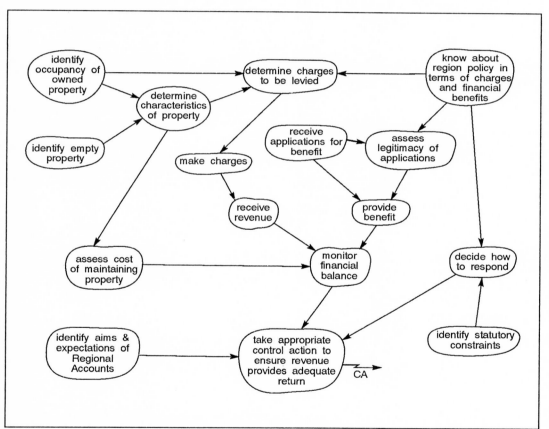

Figure 9: Conceptual model 2a derived from root definition 2a

Thus the subsystem dealing with investment has
become a system in its own right, with the system
modelled in Figure 8 as the wider system.

3.7 Summary of basic concepts

A system can be described within a hierarchy of human activity systems.

The level of detail (resolution level) at which the system is to be developed is defined through a root definition structured according to CATWOE. A logically-derived model (conceptual model) based on this root definition is a description of what the system must do to be the one defined. The conceptual model is validated against a formal systems model.

The activities in the conceptual model represent subsystems and the owner in CATWOE defines the level of the wider system. More detailed or broader models can be developed using appropriate root definitions as a means of moving down or up the systems hierarchy. At any level, there may be more than one root definition, each based on a particular W in CATWOE and leading to a different conceptual model. Since the W is different these models belong to different hierarchies.

4 SSM: general approach for computer-based information systems

4.1   Adapting SSM to IS

The methodology used in a particular situation needs to be tailored to that situation. There is not a single methodology within SSM but a variety to cope with the variety of situations themselves. This chapter describes an approach which is appropriate to an investigation of the context in which a computer-based information system might be developed.

The methodology starts with the requirement for a computer-based information system and is a five-stage process which contains extensions to the basic concepts described in Chapter 3:

- gain an understanding of the business area in which the information system is expected to provide support

- develop relevant activity models based upon significant perceptions (defined as the variable W)

- combine the above activity models into a single model, known as a consensus primary task model, and determine the information inputs and outputs required to support the activities in the model

- construct a grid to record required inputs and outputs together with those for any comparable existing procedures and map required activities against any existing organisational structures

- formulate recommendations for information system design on the basis of the comparison of information provision against requirements together with any organisational change.

4.2	Rich picture

SSM encourages the analyst to broaden the initial concern of a study away from the detail of the intended information system and towards the situation in which the information system is expected to provide useful support. The first task is to describe the situation.

In SSM, the recommendation is that this description can be expressed as a rich picture containing symbols to represent relevant components of the situation and arrows to illustrate relationships.

The analyst has complete freedom to choose those symbols and arrows that provide meaningful expression, but it is crucial that consistency of meaning is retained throughout the whole picture. An ordnance survey map is an example of a rich picture appropriate to the description of a piece of terrain and it maintains coherence through the consistency of its symbols. In addition, it transfers the meaning of its symbols from map to map, though this is not a necessary criterion for rich picture construction.

Unlike pieces of terrain, situations relevant to business contain people with attitudes, perceptions, and histories which may all affect the change processes inherent in the development of a new information system. The richness of such situations explains the term rich picture.

The example rich picture in Figure 10 shows that an individual, promoted from the role of district manager to regional director, now has as his concern the resolution of what he perceives to be district to district opposition or conflict. The key is included to define the meaning of the symbols used and is only necessary if it is desired to communicate the picture to an uninvolved third party. An example of a complete rich picture is given in Annex D.

The picture should capture the problem situation and illustrate all the elements of the problem without becoming over detailed. It is the analyst's perception of the problem.

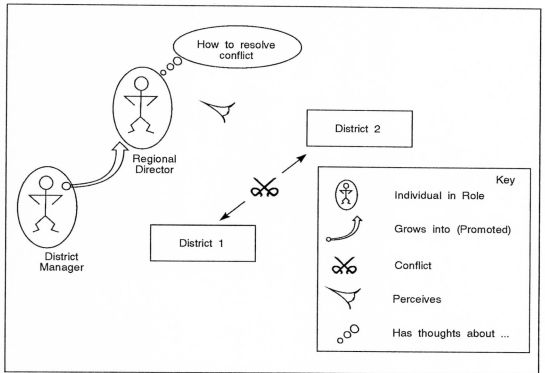

Figure 10: Fragment of a rich picture

The following are some of the questions that should be asked when constructing a rich picture:

- what business is the proposed information system to support?

- what relationships exist between the business, the information systems and other features of the environment?

- what roles or people have relationships with the situation described?

- what organisational issues are there within the situation?

Most of the benefit of the rich picture comes from its construction. Its form, whether pictorial symbols are used or text phrases linked by labelled arrows, is not particularly important. The thought processes required to develop it give rise to deep understanding of the situation and provoke thoughts about relevant human activity systems which lead to conceptual model building.

4.3   Root definitions and conceptual models

The next stage is to develop relevant issue-based and primary task root definitions, structured according to CATWOE, as described in the basic concepts chapter.

Undoubtedly, there will be information requirements arising from an issue-based analysis, but it is unlikely that an issue-based analysis would, in itself, lead to a requirement for an information system. This is because issue-based models explore a temporary situation whereas primary task models represent the long-lived on-going tasks of an organisation. Often an issue-based analysis leads to requirements for the *implementation* of a computer-based information system.

A conceptual model is derived from each root definition to represent what such a system would have to do. Conceptual models may be expanded on the basis of comparison against the real world. This comparison identifies those areas of the model that could usefully be increased in detail. These more detailed models represent higher resolution levels in the systems hierarchy. Supporting detail missing from the models may be captured in text as task descriptions.

Conceptual model building is perhaps the most creative activity of the whole process. It requires the analyst to interpret the situation expressed by the rich picture and to extract from the interpretation those descriptions of human activity systems which lead to a deep appreciation of the issues and tasks surrounding the design and implementation of the proposed information system.

4.4   Consensus primary task model and information categories

When a number of root definitions and conceptual models have been developed, the analyst has viewed the situation in a number of ways and, by working out the logical implications and comparing them with reality, derives defensible conclusions about the situation. These may be recommendations for re-structuring, the introduction of new procedures, training requirements or the development of new information systems, computerised or not.

There are several ways in which the analyst may derive conclusions about the situation. For an information-oriented proposal, the methodology requires the development of a consensus primary task model (CPTM).

4.4.1   Consensus primary task model

Each primary task model relevant to an organisational entity represents a potential role for that entity, complete company, department or individual. The reality is not any one of these models but is represented by some mixture of them. It is not possible to derive a single description which is the reality. It is possible to develop a single description, the CPTM, that may be regarded as an approximation good enough to support further development.

Primary task analysis provides the informational context for the required system. It places the specific information system within the total information requirements for the relevant area and identifies interactions with other information systems and potential users.

The CPTM is constructed from elementary primary task conceptual models which were derived from primary task root definitions. Issue-based models are not directly incorporated into the CPTM, but may define conflicts and problems that have to be recognised in creating it. Issue-based models also help formulate recommendations for information system design.

The procedure is to examine the desirability of each activity within each elementary model and assemble those that are acceptable to the users and managers concerned with the systems under investigation into a complete model. This is an interactive procedure with the users to accommodate the various viewpoints. Thus the CPTM, the resultant mixture of the individual models, represents a constructed reality.

A neutral primary task model (see Figure 11) is a description of what an organisational entity must do in order to be the kind of entity it is or needs to be. This model is universal and is hence independent of the people and the particular organisation concerned. If one regional director saw his directorate providing a safety net for people who could not afford to purchase property or to pay commercial rents and another saw his directorate actively competing in the market with property vendors and private landlords, they would agree that a regional housing directorate must have property that it rents to people in the region and collect the rents and service charges. The neutral definition achieves global consensus.

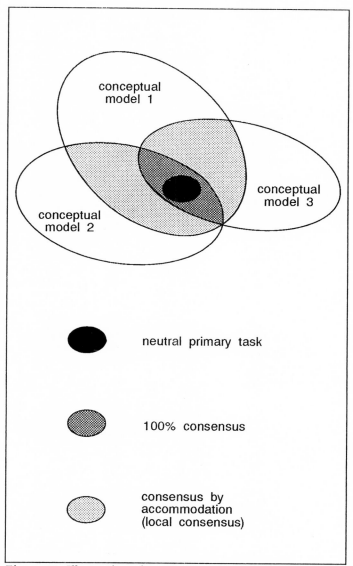

Figure 11: Illustration of consensus primary task

Usually, a neutral definition is sparse and models derived from it are sparse. A further assumption in the methodology is that less sparse models can be developed through the addition of further activities on which local consensus can be reached, ie local to the particular people and the particular organisation. The analyst develops a primary task model which includes as much consensus as can be achieved. This consensus-forming can be done in a workshop environment. The procedure is illustrated in Figure 12. The circled numbers in the diagram indicate the basic sequence. Logical dependencies have been omitted for clarity.

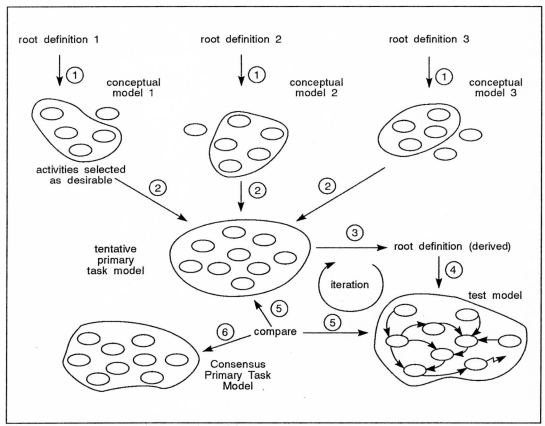

Figure 12: Consensus primary task model process

The analyst has developed three root definitions for the legitimate perceptions of the organisation. From these, conceptual models are derived describing what activities must be done for the systems to be those defined in the root definitions.

Some activities in the conceptual models are required for the neutral definition of the system and can be included in a tentative primary task model. All other activities in any of the conceptual models are examined for desirability of inclusion in the model. Desirability is subjective, decided between the analyst and the users.

Where there is 100% consensus (Figure 11) on desirability of an activity, it is included. Where there is only partial consensus on desirability, a judgment is required by analysts and users on whether to include the activity. An important criterion is whether the activity is required for logical coherence of the model.

There may be conflicts between activities from different conceptual models. For example, defining standards for rented property and ensuring that all properties offered for rent meet those standards may conflict with having available as much property as possible to meet the needs of people in the region. Additional activities concerned with resolving conflicts may have to be included in the model.

It is not always possible to resolve such conflicts in the SSM analysis. They may have to be presented as organisational issues, which give rise to information requirements, such as "what information will senior management require to enable them to decide whether to lower standards, increase the refurbishment and repair expenditure or live with longer waiting lists?"

Having produced a tentative primary task model, which may be no more than an aggregate of activities from the elementary models, the analyst must then:

- derive a root definition from the tentative model (3 in the sequence in Figure 12)

  The usual task in doing soft systems analysis is to use logic to derive a defensible model from a root definition as described in Chapter 3. In this stage, the analyst is trying to reverse the procedure and answer the question: if these activities form a conceptual model what root definition would have led to them?

- derive a coherent test model from the root definition (4 in the sequence in Figure 12)

  The procedure described in the above stage is quite difficult and so to test how good the root definition is and how coherent the set of activities in the tentative model are the more usual procedure is adopted. Thus the above root definition is taken and a model derived in the usual way (this is the test model)

- compare the test model with the tentative model (5 in the sequence in Figure 12)

  Since the more usual procedure has been adopted in the above stage the analyst is confident that the test model is a coherent model. Comparison of this model with the tentative model will indicate activities or omissions in the tentative model that make it incoherent

- modify the test model (3, 4, 5 in Figure 12).

  This is an iterative procedure. The differences observed in the above stage may either be due to actual incoherence in the tentative model or inadequacies in the root definition formed in the first stage. The differences will usually indicate which is the cause but the analyst will use judgement based on experience as a means of ensuring that the iteration is convergent and that an acceptable model (on the basis of logic) is produced.

The procedure is repeated until the test model represents the activities in the tentative model and is coherent and consistent with the derived root definition. During this procedure activities may have been added to or omitted from the original tentative model. This final version of the test model is the CPTM. Figure 13 illustrates the CPTM for the housing system.

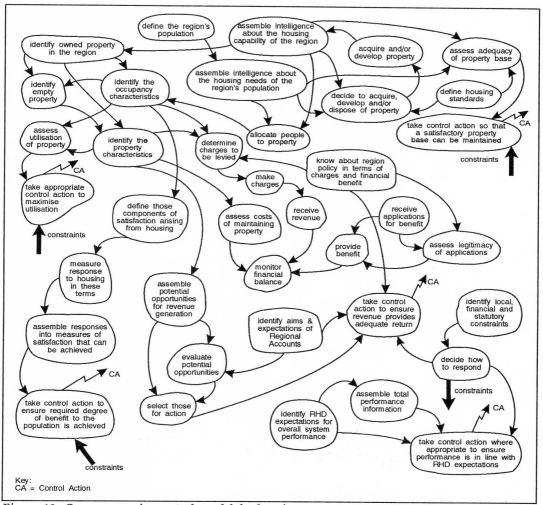

Figure 13: Consensus primary task model for housing system

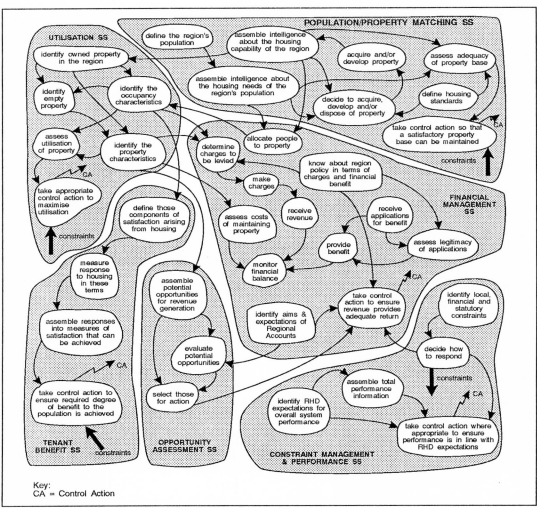

Figure 14: Partitioned CPTM for the housing system

The boundary of interest for the system under study is defined from the CPTM. The boundary may include the whole CPTM or part of it (subsystems) by partitioning the CPTM into like sets of activities. Figure 14 illustrates the CPTM given in Figure 13 partitioned into subsystems. Each activity in each subsystem is concerned with the achievement of the aim of the subsystem as represented by its title. The choice of subsystems is based upon what is useful for the analysis and is a judgement of the analyst.

4.4.2   Information categories

The CPTM is a description of the organisational entity in terms of what it is taken to do on the basis of the above analysis. Each activity in the model is necessary since it has been derived by using the procedure described in section 4.4.1. The arrows in the model represent the dependencies of activities on other activities for provision of information or resources, as described in Chapter 3.

The analysis proceeds by taking each activity in the CPTM and deriving the broad, distinct groups of information (known as information categories) needed to support the activity, together with the categories of information which are generated by doing the activity. At this stage, it is unimportant who, in terms of organisational role, does the activity.

<u>Information may be defined as data plus the meaning ascribed to it</u>. For instance, the same set of monthly sales figures may convey different information to a salesman, production manager and accountant. Information should therefore be defined in terms of the uses to which data is put.

Still at the conceptual stage, the analyst can conceive how inputs might be used in carrying out the activity and therefore can think in terms of information rather than data.

Information categories can be identified in two ways from the CPTM:

- directly, where an arrow between activities represents information

- indirectly, where an arrow between activities represents a resource. What has to be described then is the information needed by the activity to manage or account for the resource.

Further information categories required as input to activities may come from external sources.

The analyst must ask the question: "If I were to carry out a particular activity, what information would I require as input and what information would I produce as a result?" An example of this procedure is given in Figure 15, including a partially completed table in Table 3.

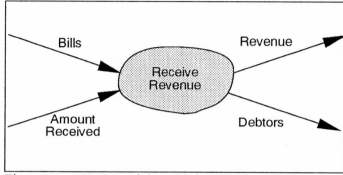

Figure 15: CPTM *activity with input and output information categories*

The activity 'Receive Revenue' in Figure 15 may be thought of as a transformation process. The arrow labelled 'Bills' represents information - what amounts were requested from what tenants, and when. For the arrow labelled 'Amount Received' what has to be described is not the actual cash received, but the information needed to account for the cash and manage it - who paid, how much was paid, when it was paid and what bill(s) the payment corresponded to.

The information categories input to and output from each activity in the CPTM are tabulated in two rows of a three row table. The third row is Measures of Performance, the information that identifies whether the activity is done well or not. This third row represents the management (as opposed to operational) information requirement.

Activity	Assess Costs of Maintaining Property	Allocate People to Property	Determine Charges to be Levied	Make Charges	Receive Revenue	Receive Application for Benefit	Assess Legitimacy of Claim	Provide Benefit	Monitor Balance
Inputs	Property List Maintenance Costs Region Boundary	Housing Application Empty Property Offer Acceptance Landlord Details Region Boundary Occupancy Priority Criteria Property Characteristics	Regional Policy Property Characteristics Occupancy Owner/ Occupier List Housing Benefit Claims	Occupancy Rent Service Charge	Bills Amounts Received	Benefit Application and Personal Details	Regional Policy Benefit Application Occupancy Debtors	Benefit Claim Personal Details Landlord Details	Revenue and Debtors Benefit Payments and Creditors Maintenance Costs
Outputs	Maintenance Costs	Allocations Occupancy Housing Applications Homeless Reports Allocation Offer	Rent Service Charge Rent Weighting	Bills	Revenue and Debtors	Benefit Application	Benefit Claim Regional Policy	Benefit Payments and Creditors	Balance Report
Measures of Performance			Admin Costs Expenditure/ Income	Shortfall in Income Expectations	Size of Debtors List				

Table 3: Information categories for financial management subsystem

4.5   Maltese cross and organisation mapping

The table of information categories represents a statement of the information requirements and hence the data needed based on the CPTM. Since information is taken to be data plus meaning, the information category represents the data content required to provide that information. The table of information categories may be used as an explicit standard against which to compare the currently available information or processed data.

4.5.1   Maltese cross

Information systems supply processed data. Since the information categories can be defined in terms of their data content (eg the information category 'personal details' could be defined in terms of the data 'name', 'age' and 'marital status'), the information required can be compared to the processed data provided and the information produced can be compared to the processed data required. The device used to perform this comparison is called the Maltese cross (Figure 16).

The top half of the Maltese cross represents a translation of the table of information categories. It therefore represents the desired situation in terms of information flows. The lower half of the Maltese cross represents the existing state of the formal information network (ie the set of information systems using defined processing methods, computer or manual). No account is taken of informal communications within the Maltese cross. The south east matrix represents the processed data produced by the current set of information systems linked to information through the information category definition. The south west matrix represents the basic data accessed and processed by the information processing procedures (IPPs).

Conclusions can be drawn about the current systems by comparing the top half to the lower half in terms of their completeness, duplications, required formality and the interactions of the proposed information system to what is already in existence. On the basis of this evidence, a proposal may be actioned for detailed design or options may be derived for further consideration.

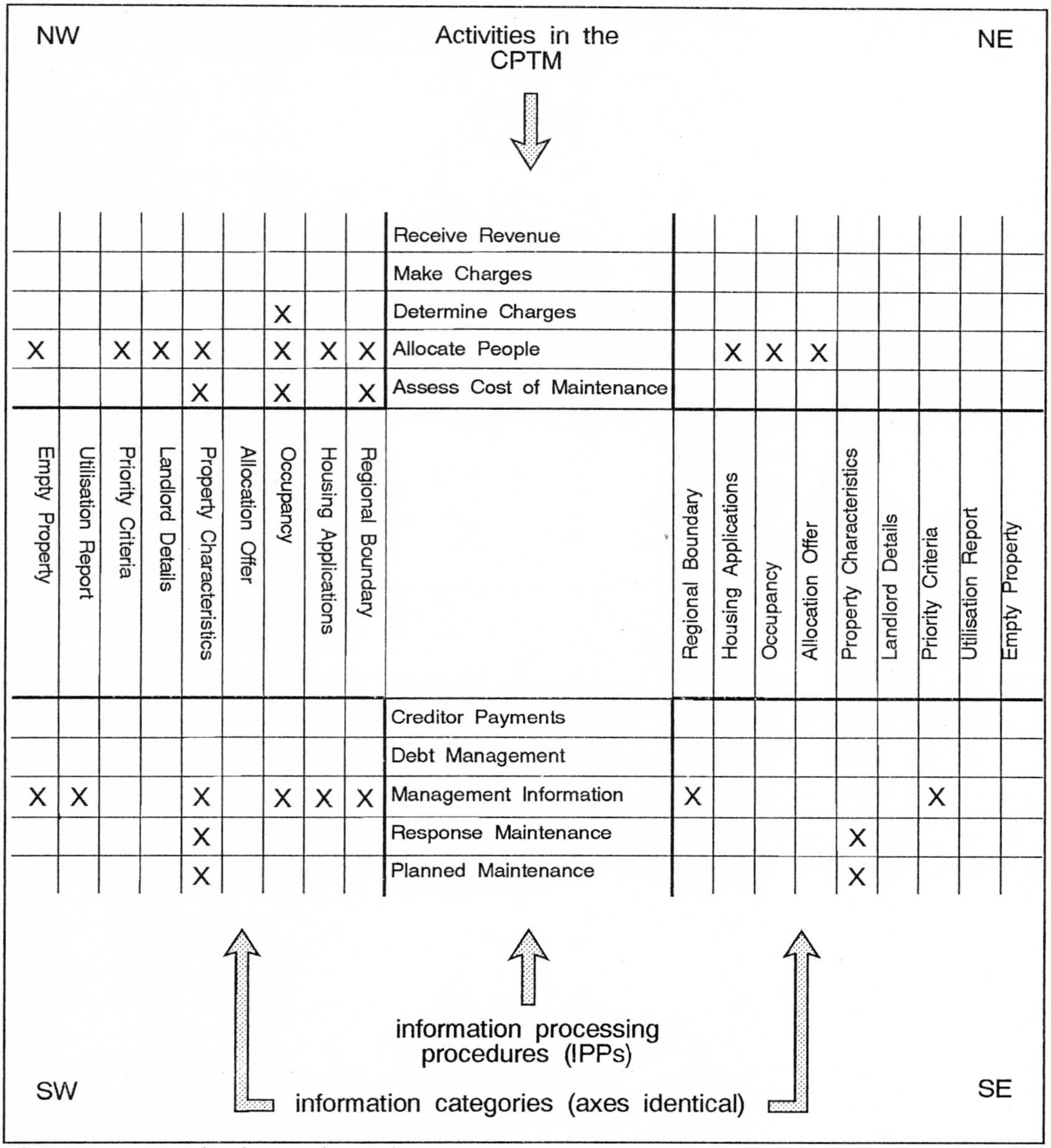

NW — Activities in the CPTM — NE

Left-side information categories (in order): Empty Property, Utilisation Report, Priority Criteria, Landlord Details, Property Characteristics, Allocation Offer, Occupancy, Housing Applications, Regional Boundary

Right-side information categories (in order): Regional Boundary, Housing Applications, Occupancy, Allocation Offer, Property Characteristics, Landlord Details, Priority Criteria, Utilisation Report, Empty Property

Top activities:

Emp.Prop	Util.Rep	Prio.Crit	Landl.Det	Prop.Char	Alloc.Off	Occup	Hous.App	Reg.Bdy	Activity	Reg.Bdy	Hous.App	Occup	Alloc.Off	Prop.Char	Landl.Det	Prio.Crit	Util.Rep	Emp.Prop
									Receive Revenue									
									Make Charges									
						X			Determine Charges									
X		X	X	X		X	X	X	Allocate People		X	X	X					
				X		X		X	Assess Cost of Maintenance									

Bottom activities:

Emp.Prop	Util.Rep	Prio.Crit	Landl.Det	Prop.Char	Alloc.Off	Occup	Hous.App	Reg.Bdy	Activity	Reg.Bdy	Hous.App	Occup	Alloc.Off	Prop.Char	Landl.Det	Prio.Crit	Util.Rep	Emp.Prop
									Creditor Payments									
									Debt Management									
X	X			X		X	X	X	Management Information	X						X		
				X					Response Maintenance				X					
				X					Planned Maintenance				X					

Arrows: information processing procedures (IPPs); information categories (axes identical)

SW — **SE**

Figure 16: Example of part of a Maltese cross

The full Maltese cross from which Figure 16 was extracted is given in Figure D3.

4.5.2 Organisation mapping

The CPTM is independent of the organisation structure. The same set of activities could be carried out under any of several possible organisation structures. However, it is necessary to know who, in terms of role within the actual organisation being investigated, is responsible for which set of activities. Users can then be properly defined and suppliers of the basic data can be identified.

The organisational mapping (Figure 17) is carried out by drawing responsibility boundaries on the CPTM around the sets of activities that represent areas of authority. These areas of authority may overlap, leading to further discussion of alternatives for re-organisation or there may be omissions, ie activities with no organisational representation. This mapping may suggest alternatives for implementation, which may give rise to further re-organisation.

The organisation mapping provides the organisational context within which the proposed information system needs to be considered. Additional users may be identified, sources of required data may be missing or inappropriately defined, and further business options may emerge.

Responsibilities for activities, or groups of activities, are defined by the organisational mapping and, although it is not explicit in the Maltese cross, the top axis can be related to organisational responsibility. Thus in the north east matrix, which represents a statement of the information categories produced by the activities, the production can be identified with appropriate people. Similarly, as the north west matrix represents those information categories used by the activities, it can be interpreted in terms of people requiring information, ie the users.

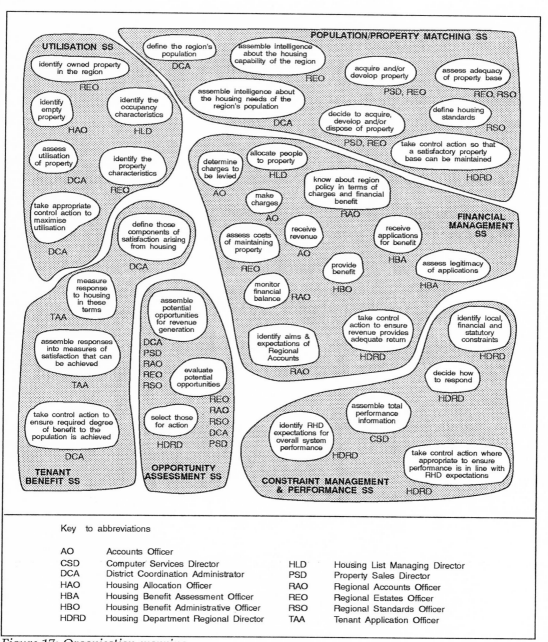

Figure 17: Organisation mapping

Key to abbreviations

AO	Accounts Officer
CSD	Computer Services Director
DCA	District Coordination Administrator
HAO	Housing Allocation Officer
HBA	Housing Benefit Assessment Officer
HBO	Housing Benefit Administrative Officer
HDRD	Housing Department Regional Director

HLD	Housing List Managing Director
PSD	Property Sales Director
RAO	Regional Accounts Officer
REO	Regional Estates Officer
RSO	Regional Standards Officer
TAA	Tenant Application Officer

It may be useful to mark problems and conflicts identified during rich picture construction on the organisation mapping, which may show up further conflicts. Figure 18 illustrates some problems and conflicts.

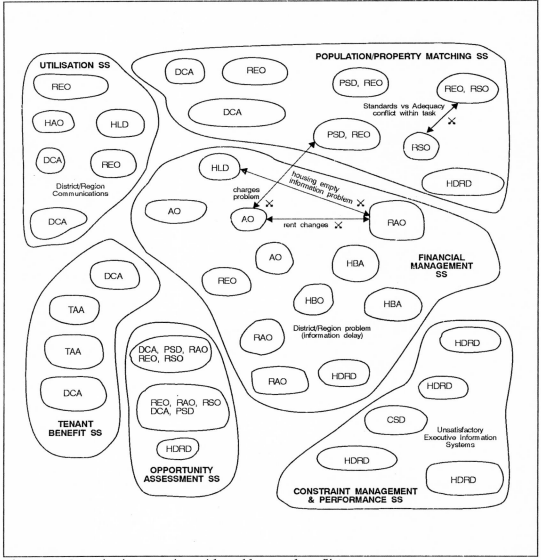

Figure 18: Organisation mapping with problems and conflicts

For instance, the Regional Standards Officer is involved in both defining housing standards and assessing the adequacy of the property base. Also, there are likely to be conflicting views when assembling and evaluating opportunities for revenue generation. The case study in Annex C gives details of other conflicts.

4.6   Summary

The five SSM stages for a general approach to computer-based information systems, from gaining an understanding of the situation to formulating recommendations for information system design, are shown in Figure 19.

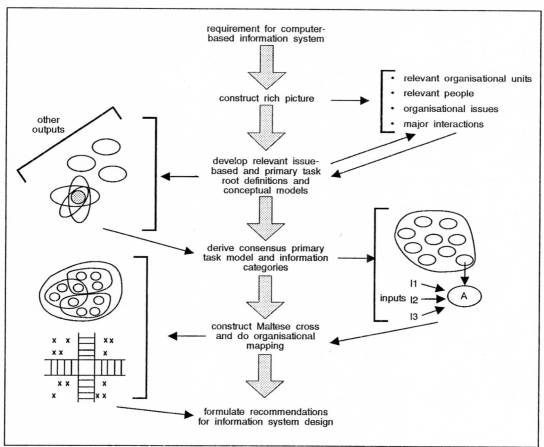

Figure 19: SSM leading to development of computer-based information system

5 SSM: application to SSADM feasibility study

5.1 General

A feasibility study is an assessment of a proposed information system to determine whether the system can effectively meet the specified business requirements of the organisation and whether a business case exists for developing such a system.

The Feasibility Study Module of SSADM is part of the core method and uses a number of its techniques. It is recommended as a preliminary to a Full Study, which involves Requirements Analysis, Requirements Specification, and Logical System Specification Modules. SSADM techniques are of principal use for the identification of information system requirements and the assessment of technical feasibility.

In this chapter, the general SSM approach to IS described in Chapter 4 is tailored to support the requirements of a feasibility study where the expectation, although not always the outcome, is the development of a computer-based information system using SSADM.

The area of business relevant to the proposed information system is explored within the context of the whole organisation to allow full investigation of potential interfaces to the system and alternative options for its design and implementation. This exploration includes a study of various peoples' perceptions, the likely impact of the system on the organisation and possible changes in related business procedures.

SSADM was designed primarily to focus on the development of the IT components pertaining to the area under study. It is important, therefore, to ensure that business objectives, benefits, and possible conflicts; together with any constraints and special monitoring and control procedures, identified during IS strategy and tactical planning are carried through into this development. Annex A details IS planning inputs to feasibility.

SSM has particular strengths in this area and therefore may be used to enhance the appropriateness and quality of the products of an SSADM feasibility study.

The section on model construction in Chapter 3 describes how activities to handle constraints, monitor performance and apply controls may be incorporated in a system. Section 4.4.1 on the construction of a consensus primary task model indicates where additional activities to resolve conflicts may be required or where additional information may be required to assist decision takers where conflicts arise.

Whilst SSM needs to be adapted to suit different situations and SSADM can be tailored for individual projects, there are three distinct approaches that can be taken to use the two together, as shown in Figure 20:

- replace the SSADM Feasibility Study Module with an SSM study

- precede the SSADM feasibility study with an SSM study

- enhance SSADM activities and products by reference to various SSM techniques.

Where an SSM study replaces the SSADM Feasibility Study Module, the products of the replacement study should include a context diagram and a catalogue of the key business requirements of the proposed system.

This approach might be relevant where there are changes to business processes, there is no current system, the technical environment is specified in strategy policies, the project is low risk, or a rapid response is required. A particular example is a requirement for a small, new system to be quickly implemented on an existing infrastructure. Here, the results of SSM analysis could be fed directly to the Requirements Analysis Module of SSADM for the definition of Business System Options and the selected option passed to the Requirements Specification Module.

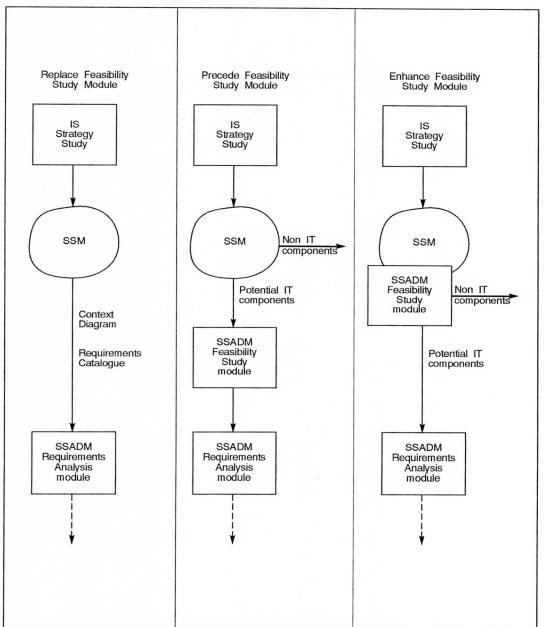

Figure 20: Three possible approaches to the use of SSM with SSADM

An SSM study which precedes an SSADM feasibility study should ensure that the project initiation input to SSADM is more closely specified.

Such an approach may be appropriate where there are conflicting interests, organisational changes are likely, the proposed system is contentious, or where the SSADM analysis is to be contracted out. For instance, a proposed system might cross functional or organisational boundaries. Conflicting interests might be accommodated as a result of using SSM or, if not, presented as organisational issues for higher management decisions before proceeding with SSADM analysis.

However, this volume focuses on the third approach of using SSM to supplement SSADM products and direct feasibility activities towards analysing information requirements which will satisfy business needs.

This approach is seen as suitable for cases where requirements may not be clear, where the proposed system is to replace or enhance an existing system, or where a new system has to interact with a number of current systems. In these situations, SSM may be used to formulate Business System Options and SSADM to analyse relevant current procedures and examine options for technical feasibility. It would be useful if the feasibility study team included members with SSADM experience who are likely to be engaged in later SSADM stages.

The guidance in this chapter assumes that if the conclusion of the study is to produce an IT system using SSADM, the products of the study should be in a form suitable for input to the Requirements Analysis Module. As with any project using the Feasibility Study Module, however, the approach taken in Stages 1 and 2 of SSADM may be modified to take account of feasibility study products.

5.2	**The enhanced approach**	There are many areas where SSM can be used in conjunction with the SSADM Feasibility Module:

- checking the validity and scope of the Project Initiation Document

- ensuring business requirements and constraints are identified and retained during requirements definition

- identifying scope and key activities for use in a Data Flow Model (DFM)

- ensuring all major interface points are identified

- assessing which aspects of the current situation require more detailed study

- ensuring a more completely scoped User Catalogue is produced

- defining mandatory requirements.

Techniques available in SSADM may be used for:

- requirements definition

- analysing existing procedures

- defining data requirements.

5.3	**SSM interface to feasibility in SSADM**	A wide range of interested parties should be involved in the feasibility study to collect all relevant details and gain general acceptance of the recommendations.

The situation is studied and documented only in sufficient detail to allow a problem definition statement to be developed and agreed with the project board, and for feasibility options to be identified.

SSM techniques which may be used are:

- rich picture building for initial scene setting

- root definition formulation and conceptual modelling for detailed understanding of different business needs

- CPTM building for a composite view of all business needs

- identification of information categories and production of information activity tables for a detailed understanding of the total information needs

- partitioning and organisational mapping to identify interfaces and potential users

- Maltese cross development and analysis for comparing required and existing information processing procedures and forming recommendations.

Several SSADM core techniques are used in a limited way, as appropriate to a feasibility study:

- requirements definition

- data flow modelling and logical data modelling for definition, in outline, of required functionality and data

- relational data analysis (RDA) for producing data models of selected information categories

- business system option and technical system option, for development and selection of feasibility options.

An outline of the way in which the two methods can complement each other is shown in Figure 21.

Note that some SSM products may need to be updated as a result of SSADM activities. The Requirements Catalogue, marked with an asterisk in Figure 21, is an SSADM product and is used to document potential high level requirements arising from initial analysis.

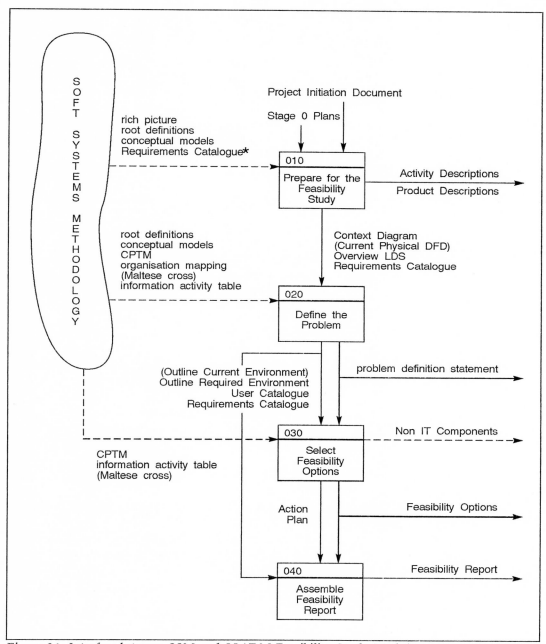

Figure 21: Interface between SSM and SSADM Feasibility Study Module

Products shown in brackets may or may not be
produced according to the specific needs of the study.

The following guidance on how the concepts outlined in Chapters 3 and 4 might interface with SSADM is split into two main sections. Section 5.4 describes the effect that SSM might have on each SSADM feasibility step whilst Section 5.5 describes the possible effect on the development of individual SSADM products.

5.4   Effect of SSM on SSADM feasibility steps

Details of the tasks and SSADM products for these steps can be found in the appropriate sections of Volume 1 of the SSADM Reference Manual.

5.4.1   Step 010 Prepare for the feasibility study

The objectives of Step 010 are to:

- ensure that the terms of reference are complete and accurate

- undertake an initial assessment of the scope and complexity of the proposed information system

- plan the rest of the feasibility study.

Figure 22 shows SSM activities that affect Step 010.

Step 010 summary

This step is principally concerned with reviewing the Project Initiation Document and IS planning inputs to ensure that the terms of reference for the study, the scope of the investigation and any relevant constraints are clearly understood. Requirements may change as a result of using SSM so any significant problems should be resolved with the appropriate authorities before proceeding any further.

The activities for development of a rich picture form a necessary first stage of investigation in which user participation is vital. The representation of the resulting product may vary from team to team, but it is important to recognise the influence of rich picture building on the SSADM technique of requirements definition in this step.

Detailed planning of the study is carried out in parallel with these activities using an approved project management method. The activities and products on which the feasibility study plans are based are identified in this step so it is here that decisions need to be made on when and how to use SSM products.

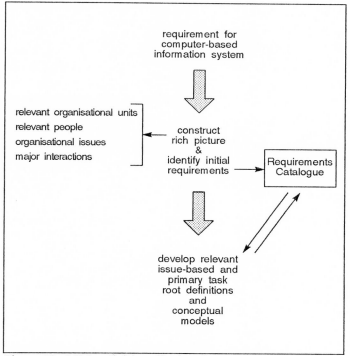

Figure 22: SSM activities affecting Step 010

Step 010 activities

Assess the complexity and scope of the system and validate the Project Initiation Document by constructing a rich picture.

Identify the high level requirements using the rich picture, root definitions and conceptual models and document these in the Requirements Catalogue. In fact, it is recommended that requirement catalogue entries are established during any initial analysis prior to commencing Step 010.

In general, functional requirements relate to primary task root definitions and non-functional requirements to issue-based root definitions at this level.

Produce an overview Logical Data Structure (LDS). Refer to a corporate data model if one exists.

Identify or confirm key entities in the LDS by studying the root definitions produced using SSM.

Assess the worth of producing a physical DFD of the current system by studying the root definitions and conceptual models. A physical DFD may help document any existing information processing procedures.

5.4.2   Step 020 Define the problem

The objectives of step 020 are to:

- obtain a more detailed understanding of the business and its information needs

- identify the problems associated with the existing situation that could potentially be resolved by the new system(s)

- identify the additional services to be provided by the new system(s)

- identify the users of the new system(s).

Figure 23 shows SSM activities that affect Step 020.

Step 020 summary

The situation has been explored by developing a number of root definitions and conceptual models related to various perceptions of the purposes and activities within the area of concern. These are now used to construct a single model, via an iterative process, which represents what the study team, in conjunction with users, are taking the situation to be. The single model is mapped against the existing organisation to highlight any organisational issues. The model is then used as a basis for defining the information required to support the area.

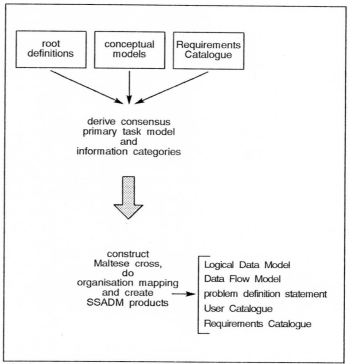

Figure 23: SSM activities affecting Step 020

The required situation is modelled at a high level. The logical processes supporting the activities in the situation are mapped against existing procedures to assess their efficiency and effectiveness. This activity highlights unsatisfactory service within the existing situation and identifies additional functions and information required in the new environment.

SSADM techniques for data flow modelling and logical data modelling are used to produce data and process models, but only to a level of detail sufficient to identify the key requirements from which feasibility options may be defined.

In the area of data flow modelling, SSM may be used in deciding the boundary and in identifying key activities to be modelled. Any work done on the Requirements Catalogue should be cross-referenced to business objectives identified using SSM and an agreement on these reached with the appropriate owner of the requirement. For further details in these areas, see sections 5.5.1 and 5.5.2 in this chapter.

Step 020 activities

Develop a consensus primary task model. Identify with the users the desirability of each activity within each conceptual model and then assemble those that are acceptable into a complete model. These key activities can be used as a start for data flow modelling. Define the boundary of interest for the proposed information system from the CPTM. This may encompass the whole CPTM or may include only a part of it, ie subsystems defined by partitioning the CPTM into like sets of activities. The boundary may define the scope for a data flow study.

Identify the information required as an input to each activity within the defined boundary of interest on the CPTM. Identify the information produced as an output from each activity. Record these information categories in an information activity table.

Identify for each activity the measures of performance, ie information which identifies whether or not the activity is done well, and add these to the information activity table. The measures form the basis for management information required to monitor the activities. Document these as service level requirements on the Requirements Catalogue.

Record on the Requirements Catalogue any operational factors such as ease of use, portability, maintainability and fast implementation as they are identified during initial SSM work.

Construct the top half of the Maltese cross using the information categories and the activities in the CPTM. This represents the required system in terms of information flows.

Identify existing information processing procedures (formalised data processing) and map these against the information flows thereby constructing the bottom half of the Maltese cross. This half represents the existing state of the formal information network or current systems. It may be useful to document this set of existing procedures in the form of a Current Physical DFD (level 1).

For each information flow, identify any omissions or potential duplication in the existing data processing and any potential interfaces with the required system by comparing the top half of the cross with the bottom half. Describe appropriate requirements in the Requirements Catalogue. This assists in producing a logical view of the existing processing procedures.

Identify who in the organisation structure, in terms of role, is responsible for which set of activities in the CPTM so that users can be defined in the User Catalogue and owners of requirements can be documented on the Requirements Catalogue. The organisation mapping may highlight actual or potential problems of overlap of responsibilities or omissions of responsibilities which should be recorded in the Requirements Catalogue.

Develop a Required LDM of the data within the boundary of interest.

Develop an initial Required DFM for the system of interest. Transfer activities directly from the CPTM to the DFDs interpreting each activity as a process to support the human activity. The organisation mapping can be used in identifying those external entities in a DFD which have direct responsibility for the activity that the process is supporting. Data stores may be identified from a study of the information categories on the information activity table.

Compare data flows drawn in the DFDs with information categories from information activity tables in order to converge to a consistent set of flows to be used in the DFM. This Required System DFM is used in the selection of options.

Prepare a problem definition statement summarising the requirements and assessing priorities in relation to business objectives. Agree the problem definition statement with the project board.

5.4.3 Step 030 Select Feasibility Options

The objectives of step 030 are to:

- develop a range of Feasibility Options that meet defined requirements and from which users can make a selection

- gain user ownership of the results of the study by presenting the Feasibility Options to the project board and assisting in the selection of the preferred option

- recommend a preferred project or projects to implement each Feasibility Option

- produce outline development plans for the selected project(s).

Step 030 summary

Feasibility Options, possible logical solutions to the requirements described in the problem definition statement, are formed by combining Business System Options (BSOs) with Technical System Options (TSOs).

Tasks for this step are given in Volume 1 of the SSADM Reference Manual. The results of SSM primary task analysis and issue-based analysis can be used in defining BSOs and TSOs respectively. The CPTM and Maltese cross will have been used to determine functional requirements whilst measures of performance in the information activity table will have been used to compile non-functional requirements. Any constraints imposed by strategy documents will have been incorporated in the Requirements Catalogue.

After discussion with the users, a short list of composite options is presented to the project board for the selection of the preferred option. The ways in which SSM can assist the choice and presentation of composite options are described in section 5.5.5.

5.4.4	Step 040 Assemble the Feasibility Report	The objectives of step 040 are to:

- ensure the integrity of the feasibility study

- publish the Feasibility Report.

Step 040 summary

This step completes the feasibility study. The tasks, given in Volume 1 of the SSADM Reference Manual, are concerned with checking the consistency of the products of the study and assembling them into the Feasibility Report. This report, together with any other management reports that are required, are published to organisation standards.

Quality criteria for individual SSADM products are defined as part of a Product Description given in Volume 4 of the SSADM Reference Manual. Similar descriptions for the results of SSM analysis are given in Annex D of this volume. However, the products need to be checked against one another for consistency.

5.5 Effect of SSM on SSADM feasibility products

The areas of SSADM discussed here are:

- requirements definition, specifically the Requirements Catalogue

- data flow modelling

- logical data modelling

- dialogue design, specifically the User Catalogue

- BSO/TSO and their use in composite options

- activity and product descriptions.

5.5.1 Requirements definition

The purpose of requirements definition is to identify and specify requirements so that any proposed system meets the needs of users and the business as a whole. Functional requirements, describing features and facilities required of a new system, and non-functional requirements relating to them, such as service levels and constraints, are recorded in the Requirements Catalogue (see Figure 24).

The Requirements Catalogue establishes common understanding between users and analysts by bringing together their views of the requirements. Many of the entries recorded on the Requirements Catalogue during feasibility study are enhanced by the use of the SSM approach to analysing a business or organisation. These entries are used in step 030 to derive a number of options, and a clear indication of priority, benefits and impact on other requirements assist in the choice.

This is an area in which SSM has a significant contribution to make. Any activity forming the neutral primary task model will give rise to a mandatory requirement. Other activities included in the CPTM will generate either mandatory or desirable requirements. An examination of the partitioned CPTM will help decide the priority.

Requirements Catalogue Entry

SSPM
VERSION4

System	Author	Date	Version	Status	Page	of

Source	District Coordination Administrator	Priority	Mandatory	Owner	Housing Directorate	Requirement ID	RI

Functional requirement

To produce a report showing an assessment of Property Utilisation

Non-functional requirement(s)

Description	Target value	Acceptable range	Comments
Report frequency	Daily		
Run time	20 minutes		
latest finish	by start of working day		
security	Data Protection Act to be adhered to	Mandatory	

Benefits

Will provide District Coordination Administrator with information to improve decision making

Comments/suggested solutions

Related documents

Related requirements

Resolution

Figure 24: Sample Requirements Catalogue entry for property utilisation report

ENTRY	DESCRIPTION OF ENTRY	SSM INFLUENCES
Source	enter the source(s) of the requirement. This may be a person, document or SSADM product	rich picture root definition
Priority	enter a priority for the requirement, defined by the user and described as high/low or mandatory/desirable/optional	neutral primary task model CPTM Partitioned CPTM
Owner	enter the user or user organisation with ownership and responsibility for negotiation about the requirement	often the owner as defined in CATWOE analysis
Functional requirement	enter a description of a facility or feature that is required	rich picture root definitions CPTM Maltese cross
Non-functional requirement	enter a description of non-functional requirements and where possible identify target value, acceptable range (including any maximum or minimum values) and any qualifying comments	information activity table
Benefits	briefly describe the benefits expected from meeting the requirement	root definitions information activity table
Comments/ suggested solutions	note any possible solutions to the requirement and any general comments	issue-based root definitions
Related documents	enter a reference to any related documents, for example, user documentation, DFD, PID	relevant SSM document
Related requirements	if different requirements influence each other or conflict they should be cross referenced so any variation in one can be assessed with reference to the impact on the other	conflicts from rich picture and organisational mapping
Resolution	make a note of how a requirement is resolved; for example, by reference to a Function Definition. If a decision is made not to pursue a requirement, for example, following BSOs, reasons should be recorded	record decisions as to whether this requirement is frozen or its resolution is to be determined via SSADM or some other means

Table 4: SSM influences on entries in the Requirements Catalogue

Benefits may be discerned initially from root definitions and later from measures of performance in the information activity table. Conflicts are recorded on the rich picture and organisational mapping. Activities to resolve conflicts may give rise to further requirements. Issue-based analysis may also surface conflicts or suggest possible solutions to requirements. Table 4 summarises where SSM might contribute.

It is strongly recommended that the Requirements Catalogue be the major link between the two methods. Key entries should be created and updated whether using SSM or SSADM. Any entries in this catalogue which cannot be satisfied using SSADM should be annotated as such at the appropriate point and dealt with in alternative ways.

5.5.2 Data flow modelling

A number of types of DFDs are produced within the SSADM Feasibility Study Module, documenting both current and required views of the area under study.

SSM conceptual models concentrate initially on activities rather than on data flows. Subsequently, input and output information flows required for those activities are identified and defined. The approach can be used to direct the scope of DFDs and ensure that they focus on the key information processes necessary to support the business.

Where there is apparent duplication between required activities and current processes, SSM can be used to identify a context diagram giving the boundary for a current system DFD. Where there is little overlap between required activities and existing processes, a CPTM and associated information categories can be used to produce a Required System DFD. The SSADM technique of logicalisation may need to be carried out on the data stores of the Required System DFD to ensure it is in a form consistent with its use in later stages of SSADM.

The reason for producing a Required System DFD is to document the elementary processing and to help identify the following items as inputs to more detailed techniques later in SSADM:

- functions, for subsequent use in Function Definition

- events

- user roles

- dialogues and input/output flows.

While the DFMs of SSADM and the conceptual models of SSM have some common ground, there are also some significant differences between them. These differences need to be understood if the two types of models are to be used together.

The key differences are that:

- arrowed lines denote data flows on a DFD but logical dependencies on a conceptual model

- DFDs are derived from a study of flows, whereas conceptual models are built from a study of activities

- data flow diagram analysis begins with a study of the current situation, whereas conceptual modelling concentrates on what people perceive ought to be done

- in data flow modelling, data stores in the current system are considered initially whereas in SSM, high level information categories needed to carry out activities are identified.

SSM can be used in the initial development of DFDs by identifying relevant processes and external entities. Information categories can be used in the identification of data stores and flows.

There is often no need to focus on the current system in detail and as a consequence, the Required System DFD is more valuable in the later detailed stages of analysis and design.

The procedure for developing a DFD in outline is that:

- DFD processes are defined from activities in the CPTM. They are grouped by CPTM subsystem to define lower level DFDs

- information activity tables assist in identifying input, output, and data stores

- organisation mapping identifies system users. These are sources (external entities) of many input data flows and destinations of some output data flows. This in turn helps identify the system boundary.

Comparison between the upper and lower halves of the Maltese cross indicates whether processes are present in the current system and can be compared, in function and performance, with their equivalents in the new system or are new requirements. A current physical DFD may be produced to assist the construction of the lower half of the Maltese cross.

Data flow model components

In Step 020, a DFD of the required environment is produced from the CPTM, with organisation mapping, and the Maltese cross.

The DFD components are:

- external entities

- data stores and data flows

- processes.

External entities

These may be determined initially from actors, as in CATWOE elements for root definitions, whose role can be split into activities that remain outside the scope of any automated information system and those that could be replaced in the new system. The external role is represented as an external entity.

People or other systems outside the scope of the feasibility study who provide information to or receive information from the activities in the CPTM are also represented as external entities.

Organisation mapping can identify further external entities which may receive information from a new system.

Data stores and data flows

SSM gives little formal assistance in the identification of data stores and flows. However, a study of information activity table inputs and outputs may be useful in ensuring that no major data stores or flows are omitted from the Required System DFD.

Each input in an information activity table should be categorised as internal or external to the scope of the study in question. Those that are internal assist in the identification of the data stores needed by the processes in the Required System DFM and subsequently can be cross-referenced against the entities on the LDS to ensure that data is not duplicated.

Those inputs that are external assist in the identification of data flows from external entities.

Data stores may be:

- those that model a store or reservoir of a resource or capacity for a service, for example, properties available for letting

- those that record the system's expectations of responses to outputs it has sent to external entities, for example, bills due for payment

- those that model external entities with which the system communicates. They contain reference information, such as names and addresses, and often contain state information, such as account balance and arrears balance.

Processes

Having identified the external entities and main data flows, it is now possible to produce a context diagram (see Figure 25) of the scope to be studied using the SSADM technique of data flow modelling.

High level DFD processes within this context diagram may be derived from the SSM activities in the CPTM and information activity tables. These processes may be activities in the CPTM that are themselves information processing activities.

They may also arise from information processing support for activities in the CPTM that handle resources and services. These are implied when defining the corresponding information categories for the Maltese cross. For example, a CPTM activity 'Receive Revenue' might have the information categories 'amount received' as an input and 'revenue' as an output. The information categories are not the actual payments, but information about them. Thus the DFD process is not to receive the revenue, but to post the payments made to tenants' accounts and produce reports on revenue received. The actual receipt of revenue ie handling cash, cheques and depositing them in the bank, is outside the boundary of the DFD. In specifying the DFD process in this way, the internal and external roles of the actors are also identified.

A third kind of process may be required for the production of management information, the measures of performance row in the information activity table, where this cannot be produced as a side effect of the CPTM-based processes.

Using SSM in this manner ensures that the context diagram includes only those processes which help deliver business benefits. This makes better use of SSADM resources and should reduce time spent during Stages 1 and 2.

Figure 25 shows a context diagram for a proposed housing system which encompasses the utilisation and financial management subsystems of the partitioned consensus primary task model in Figure 14. The external entities in the context diagram were derived from organisation mapping details given in Figure 17. Data flows were derived from inputs and outputs given in Tables 3 and 5.

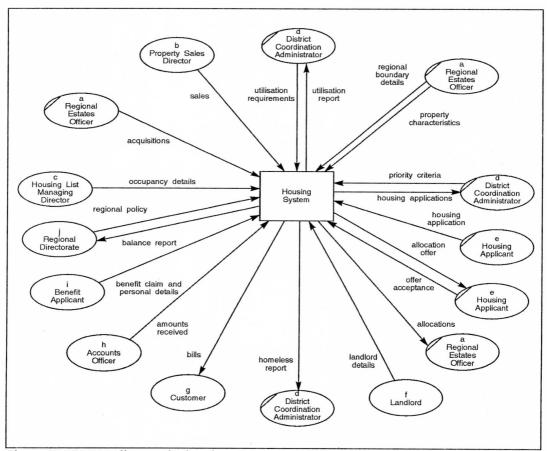

Figure 25: Context diagram for housing system

Level 1 DFD processes 'Monitor Property Utilisation' and 'Monitor Financial Information', corresponding to utilisation and financial management subsystems respectively, are shown in Figure 26.

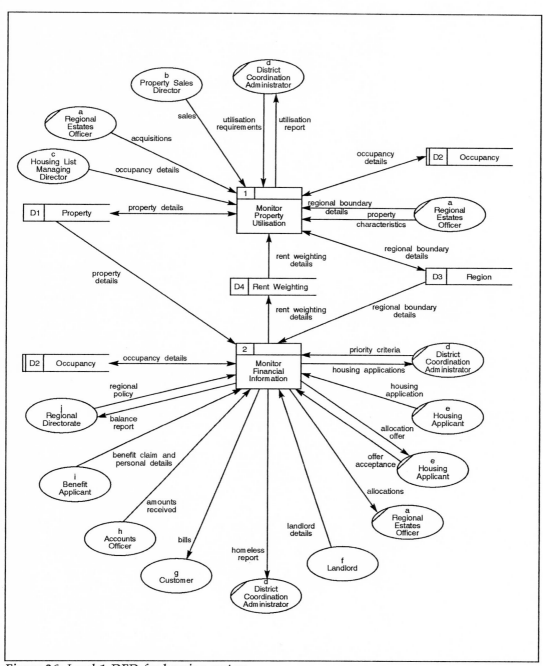

Figure 26: Level 1 DFD for housing system

Activity	Identify Owned Property in the Region	Identify Occupancy Characteristics	Identify Empty Property	Assess Utilisation of Property	Identify Property Characteristics
Inputs	Region Boundary	Occupancy	Property List	Property Characteristics	Property List
	Acquisitions	Regional Boundary	Occupancy	Empty Property Report	Property Characteristics
	Sales			Occupancy	Rent Weighting
	Property List			Regional Boundary	Regional Boundary
				Utilisation Requirements	
Outputs	Property List	Occupancy	Empty Property Report	Utilisation Report	Property Characteristics
	Owner/ Occupier List				Regional Boundary

Table 5: Inputs and outputs for utilisation subsystem

Table 5 shows inputs and outputs for utilisation subsystem activities. These activities appear as processes in the Level 2 DFD in Figure 27.

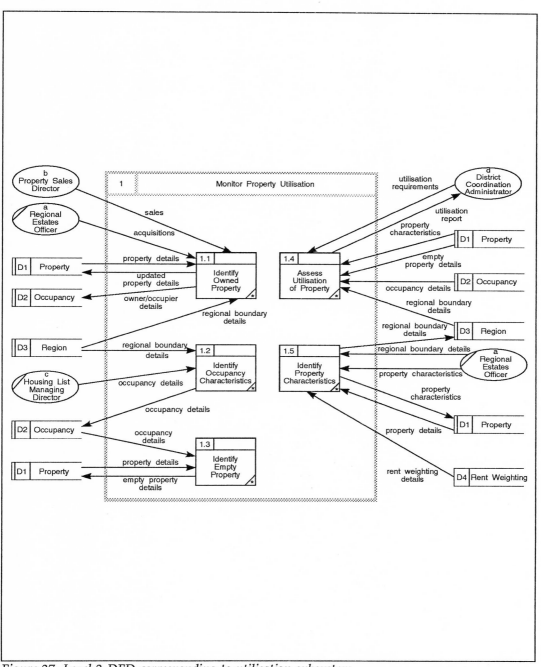

Figure 27: Level 2 DFD corresponding to utilisation subsystem

5.5.3 Logical data modelling

The SSADM approach to logical data modelling should remain unchanged as SSM concentrates on the information needs of a system rather than its data content. However, key entities and relationships can be identified during the production of an overview LDS by a study of root definitions and the sources and recipients of information categories on the information activity table.

Candidate entities include:

- customers, as in CATWOE analysis

- types of resource, including products and services, controlled by activities in the CPTM

- types of location at which resources are available

- suppliers of resources.

In addition, the SSADM technique of relational data analysis (RDA) may be carried out on selected SSM information categories to assist the production of an initial LDS.

5.5.4 User Catalogue

The User Catalogue defines the on-line users of the required system. Initial job titles and activity descriptions can be identified via the actor and transformation elements respectively of root definitions. If actors have not been explicitly stated in a root definition, then job titles may be determined later when assigning responsibilities for activities during organisational mapping.

5.5.5 Composite options

Prior to selection of options in step 030, the use of SSM will have helped to ensure that the Requirements Catalogue and Required System DFM are biased towards business needs, particularly with reference to priorities and benefits on the Requirements Catalogue.

SSM also has the following parts to play in the presentation and choice of options:

- the CPTM identifies areas of activity which should be addressed in the majority of options presented

- the Maltese cross identifies the amount of overlap between the required system and the current information processing system. This helps define how much detailed work needs to be done in each option in terms of current system investigation

- SSM also identifies areas of conflict which the analyst needs to be aware of prior to presentation of options

- measures of performance required have been documented on the information activity table and the Requirements Catalogue and these are used in both the BSO and the TSO parts of Step 030

- areas of impact have to be considered particularly with regard to interfaces, organisational changes and improved manual procedures.

5.5.6 Activity and product descriptions

Activity and product descriptions needed for the particular project being undertaken are produced in Step 010 of SSADM. Thus thought has to be given as to where and when SSM should be used and to what level of detail SSADM products need be taken. For instance, instead of developing a current system DFM, a context diagram may suffice.

5.6	**Effect of feasibility on Requirements Analysis Module**	In SSADM, the decision to use the Feasibility Study Module always has an effect on the way Stages 1 and 2 are dealt with in the Full Study. Part of the Feasibility Report contains the project plan and this should outline the activities and products envisaged in the Requirements Analysis Module. Clearly, this is influenced by the actual products resulting from the feasibility study and the level of detail to which they have been defined.

This area should be discussed with the project manager at step 110 in the Requirements Analysis Module in order to produce activity and product descriptions for the initial part of the Full Study.

6 Summary and conclusions

This volume is primarily intended for members of a feasibility study team who wish to use Soft Systems Methodology (SSM) to complement activities supported by SSADM techniques. It describes the general concepts of SSM and how they can be adapted to information systems before considering interfaces with SSADM.

The aim is to show how SSM can make better use of SSADM resources in problem definition, save time in subsequent requirements analysis and specification, and lead towards the development of applications which more fully satisfy business needs.

SSM is an organised way of reaching value judgements via a process of analysis that is explicit and defensible. It assists the analyst to select the most relevant set of perceptions from the many different and often conflicting understandings and views which may be held by interested parties on what an organisation's main purpose and objectives ought to be.

Separate, logical models of system activities are developed and validated to reflect those perceptions and gain a full insight into the business area under study. Activities from the individual models are combined to form a single model which should accommodate the various perceptions. The operational and management information required to support the system represented by this consensus model is derived from the activities within the model.

The model and its associated information requirements now form a basis from which to compare what is required with what is currently provided. Options for the design and implementation of an effective, efficient system to meet the requirements of the particular part of the organisation may then be formulated.

Because SSM takes into account different views of what the organisation is trying to achieve, it may be used where business requirements are unclear, interests conflict, or the proposed system is contentious.

SSM also may be applied to good effect where there are to be changes in organisational structure or business processes since IS requirements are derived by means which are independent of any formal organisation structure and independent of any existing manual or automated procedures for processing information.

Both SSADM and SSM can be tailored to suit an organisation's particular requirements. Used together, their relative strengths may be exploited to complement one another. Thus, SSM might replace the SSADM Feasibility Module in circumstances where there are no existing systems and precede it where organisational issues or conflicting interests are a concern.

In situations where there are existing systems and requirements are unclear, SSM can be used to explore interfaces to other areas of the organisation and analyse information requirements whilst SSADM techniques are employed to analyse current procedures and data requirements that are relevant to the proposed system.

As they are established between analysts and users, requirements should be recorded on the Requirements Catalogue, an SSADM product, which then forms a link between SSM and SSADM activities. The two types of activities should be coordinated using a recognised project management method.

Whilst the conceptual models of SSM and the Data Flow Diagrams of SSADM may bear a superficial resemblance to one another, it is as well to be aware of their differences if they are to be compared. However, a Context Diagram, for instance, may be derived from a consensus primary task model and its associated information requirements when thought is given to who, in terms of organisational role, might assume responsibility for sets of activities in the model.

Those who wish to use the guidance in this volume are advised to have had formal training in SSM and to have support from an experienced practitioner before applying the approach to an SSADM feasibility study.

Annex A: IS planning inputs

A.1   IS strategy planning

IS strategy planning is a cyclical process and the policies and plans that result from it evolve with time as studies are completed and applications implemented.

Strategy planning for IS involves:

- understanding the current business environment including existing IS, *where are we now?*

- identifying business direction, *where do we want to be?*

- identifying the systems needed to meet these business objectives, *how do we get there?*.

The IS strategy highlights possible options for introducing systems and gives an indication of the cost and time scale for development and introduction. However, the extent of this work is likely to be limited to a level sufficient only for determining the priorities and the broad order of cost.

There are a number of techniques which can assist strategic thinking and planning: they support identification of issues, aims, objectives, context, influences, strengths, weaknesses and opportunities. Overviews of these techniques, including SSM, are described in Annex D of the IS Guide A2: *Strategic Planning for Information Systems.*

The IS strategy includes various documents which may be relevant for a feasibility study. Ideally, appropriate details will have been added to the Project Initiation Document:

- IS strategy statement

- management and technical policies

- IS strategy planning interim products.

The IS strategy statement gives a business overview of the information systems which are needed during the next five to ten years. It paints a broad picture of what is to be achieved and the benefits likely to result. It should indicate how the strategy is to be monitored and specify appropriate measures of achievement.

Management and technical policies provide a framework of guidance for those involved in implementing the strategy.

IS strategy planning interim products include contrasting models of the business and a review of existing systems. Their value depends on how up-to-date they are.

The interface between IS strategy planning and SSADM is described in the Information Systems Engineering volume: *SSADM in an IS Strategy Environment.*

A.2   **Tactical planning**

Tactical planning is the process of turning an IS strategy into more detailed and realisable plans of action. It focuses on the next 12-18 months. Its purpose is to refine the IS Strategy into specific manageable programmes of work, and to ensure that resources are allocated between competing demands as effectively as possible. As with strategy planning, tactical planning is a cyclical process which can evolve or change with time.

The programmes of work identified in the strategy are broken down into specific projects. The project portfolio gives details of business applications, the infrastructure developments to underpin them and other activities that have to be undertaken to progress the IS strategy.

The project portfolio should contain:

- a brief description of the project or study

- details of the project sponsor and who is responsible for carrying out the project or study

- project or business objectives, outline systems definition or terms of reference

- details of any dependencies between this and other projects or external events

- notes of any constraints and of any special management, control or monitoring procedures

- copies of the project plans and resources profile.

A.3   Programme management

CCTA is to produce a guide to programme management which includes a description of programme level feasibility studies.

A.4   Project planning

At the lowest level, individual projects and studies need to be planned. The tactical plan has taken the programmes of work of the IS strategy and refined them into a number of specific projects to be carried out to a specific timetable. Each project has its own project board and project manager who are responsible respectively for the overall control and day-to-day management of the project.

The results of each project are fed back into tactical and strategy planning.

Annex B: Elements of a soft systems approach

What features of a soft systems approach may be regarded as mandatory? If an analyst adopts a soft systems approach, what minimum set of ideas must be used? What kind of performance assessment is possible?

B.1   Mandatory elements

In summary, the mandatory elements of a soft systems approach are:

- consideration given to multiple Weltanschauungen (Ws)

- explicit root definition and associated conceptual models

- declared methodology.

Consideration of multiple perceptions

Given the importance of the multiple Ws in the situation, the analyst must develop more than one model of a human activity system. It is this variable (W) which makes the application of a soft systems methodology appropriate and important.

Explicit root definition and associated conceptual models

In relation to each model a root definition must be formulated and structured according to the mnemonic CATWOE. It is this root definition which determines the particular set of activities and their linkage which constitute a complete description of what the system must do to be the one defined. Any detailed elaboration of activities within the model also requires the formulation of an appropriate root definition. Consistency of W must be maintained as more detailed models are produced since they represent a defensible expansion of the first root definition.

Declared methodology

Since there is a need for flexibility in the approach adopted there is not a standard soft systems methodology, however the particular methodology to be used needs to be declared. It may change as the analysis progresses but such changes need to be the result of conscious decisions to do so. The learning that is achieved from this process can be articulated if the methodology is explicit at all times.

B.2 Additional elements

Depending upon the particular methodology used, a number of other elements may be useful and can be incorporated. For SSM analysis that is expected to lead to implementation of a computer-based information system, these are:

- rich picture building as a representation of the problem situation

- a CPTM which represents a taken as given activity description of an organisation or area within an organisation

- an organisation map which describes the allocation of responsibilities for activities within the CPTM based upon a current or potential organisation structure

- a Maltese cross, which enables comparison to be made between information support requirements, on the basis of a CPTM, and the current real world data processing provision.

It is worth adding that SSM is not a replacement for other approaches but is an enhancement of them. Systems engineering and other techniques can be used, as appropriate, within a soft systems framework.

B.3 Performance assessment

Performance assessment related to a methodology is extremely difficult. It is not independent of the practitioner and hence 'who uses it' is as important as 'what it is'. This applies to any methodology and not just to SSM. Client acceptance is an obvious measure but it is a measure of the outcome of a project. It is a measure of the acceptability of the result not the method of analysis leading to the result.

To assess the process of analysis being undertaken, it is useful to examine the mandatory elements and derive measures of performance appropriate to them and then to assess the performance of any additional elements being used. These measures are not quantifiable but represent features to be considered when undertaking an audit of an SSM project.

Range of systems considered

An analysis based on a single system is not acceptable unless it is a consensus primary task system derived from a number of other primary task systems. Thus an indication of the range and thoroughness of the exploration is in terms of the number of systems considered, the significance of the differences between them and the mix of issue-based and primary task systems defined.

Conceptual model

A formal systems model (FSM) has been derived as a model of any human activity system. This is the equivalent of CATWOE for the root definition. A particular conceptual model can be validated against this.

Root definition/ conceptual model relationship

A process of logic has been used to derive the conceptual model from the set of words and structure of the root definition. Thus if the root definition states what the system is, the conceptual model defines what the system has to do to be the one defined. This logical process must be defended against other analyst or peer group members.

Intellectual structure (methodology)

The process of problem solving is describable as a human activity system. Thus, the set of purposeful activities required to derive recommendations relevant to an initial set of concerns can be derived from a problem solving (issue-based) root definition. This process of derivation provides coherence in the set of problem solving activities and their resultant structure.

Rich picture

The construction of a rich picture of a situation which is problematical allows interpretations, assumptions and knowledge about the situation to be made explicit and shared. This leads to a common group understanding and interpretation of the situation to be analysed.

Consensus primary task model (CPTM)

In deriving a CPTM, the range of views (Ws) of the situation relevant to a given population of individuals has been explored as separate systems models. The process of bringing them together to a single model is a process of debate in which the different Ws can be accommodated. This is a successful process if the same population have commitment to the model, indicated by its acceptability to them.

Organisation map

Since there is a maintenance of the distinction between conceptual models and the real world, all of the models are independent of any organisation structure that might exist in the real world. A CPTM is a description of what the real world situation is taken to be. Hence it should be possible to relate the activities within it to what people do in the situation. An organisation map is an explicit relationship of this kind. It defines 'who does what' and 'who is responsible for what' in the situation. The reliability of the map is a function of the degree of participation of the people concerned.

Maltese cross

There are two stages in the construction of a Maltese cross. The first is the formulation of an information table, which represents the top half of the Maltese cross. The usefulness of the Maltese cross is dependent upon the completeness of this table since it defines the information support needed by the set of activities in the CPTM.

The second stage is to complete the bottom half of the Maltese cross by entering the formal data-processing systems that exist in the situation relevant to the CPTM. Since the resolution level of the CPTM is based upon the way the analysis has been carried out, it bears little relation to the ways in which the formal data-processing systems were designed. They were probably designed over an extended period of time and with little dependence on each other. They, therefore, need to be ranked according to the resolution level of the CPTM to ensure that nothing is omitted when completing the bottom half of the Maltese cross. If this can be achieved, the comparison of the top half to the bottom half yields a true assessment of 'what is provided' in terms of 'what is required'.

B.4 Summary of performance assessment

The above performance assessment considerations may be summarised in terms of those elements that are mandatory and those which are additional as shown in Table B1.

	SSM elements	Performance measures
Mandatory	Range of systems considered	How many, differences issue-based/primary task mix
	Root definitions	CATWOE check
	Conceptual models	Formal system model check
	Root definition/conceptual model relationship	Defensibility
	Intellectual structure (methodology)	Coherence
Additional	Rich picture	Commonality of interpretation within analyst group
	CPTM	Acceptability to the relevant population
	Organisation map	Existence/degree of participation
	Maltese cross	- Information table - Lower axis Completeness appropriate to the ranking

Table B1: Summary of performance assessment

In the analysis of a situation which itself is soft, there are unlikely to be quantifiable measures which allow for unquestionable assessment of the thinking process. At best the overall quality of the analysis is based upon judgments related to qualitative assessments. However, the list in Table B1 provides indicators of what to look for.

Annex C: Case study

The examples used throughout the volume are based upon a housing region study similar to that used in the SSADM Reference Manual. The housing region is organised as shown in Figure C1.

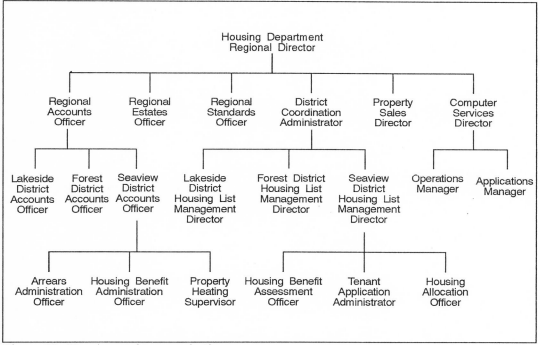

Figure C1: Housing region organisation

The Housing Department administers property, housing benefit and housing allocations. The District Accounts Departments, located within the Regional Offices and thus remote from other district functions, keep manual files of tenants and rents due which duplicate those held by Housing List management. Accounts and Housing Allocations have to be informed separately of any rent increases which has led to tenants being notified of one amount and being charged another.

Housing benefit is assessed and administered manually.

The computer system for housing waiting lists is old, slow and at the limit of its capacity. The lists are not accurate and have to be adjusted manually for reports.

Empty properties should be allocated within one month unless maintenance is needed. However, some remain empty for longer periods while applications are sorted. Also, when a tenant transfers to another district, the previous district is not immediately informed and so is unaware that a property has been vacated.

Regional management is concerned about an increase in the number of tenancies being rejected. It is not known whether applicants are becoming more selective or the accommodation being offered is obviously unsuitable.

The Regional Accounts Department does not get to know about sales of property which incur service charges for at least four months. Service charges then have to be back-dated and recouped.

The Property Heating Supervisor may not know about sales or acquisitions of property until three to four months after the transactions, which means projected costs may be out of date.

The Regional Accounts Department has just had new General Ledger, Creditor Payments and Bank Reconciliation systems installed. There are also Housing Acquisition and Sales, Response Maintenance and Planned Maintenance systems.

The population is growing and there is pressure from the Government to reduce the number of homeless within the region.

Part of the IS strategy was to replace the existing waiting list system with the inclusion of housing benefit so as to integrate with the new systems.

There is a need for a feasibility study on replacement of the existing computer systems within the District Housing Departments.

Annex D: SSM product descriptions

D.1 Conceptual model

Purpose

To record what a system must do in order for it to be as described in its root definition.

Composition

The minimum necessary set of activities described in irregularly shaped boxes and linked by arrows depicting logical dependencies.

The boxes may be numbered for reference purposes and for reflecting levels without implying any sequence of activities.

Derivation

Root definition

Quality

Criteria:

1 Do activities included in the model relate to words used in the root definition from which it is derived?

2 Does the description of an activity begin with a verb in the imperative?

3 Are monitor and control activities included?

4 Are there activities to acquire and deploy resources?

5 Are the activities described at the same level of detail?

6 Do the activities and their logical dependencies form a coherent set?

External dependencies

Interested parties available for involvement in validation exercise.

References

Conceptual model building   Section 3.5
Consensus primary task model building   Section 4.4.1

An example conceptual model is given in Figure D1

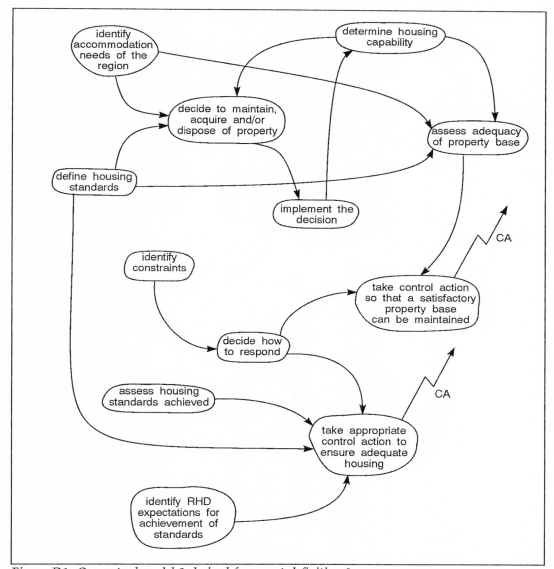

Figure D1: Conceptual model 3 derived from root definition 3

Root definition 3   "A Regional Housing Directorate owned system to
                           maintain and develop its property base so that
                           adequate standards of housing can be achieved in
                           relation to the accommodation needs of the region
                           whilst recognising local, financial and statutory
                           constraints."

D.2   Consensus primary task model

Purpose	To record what a system must do in order for it to be as described in its root definition.
Composition	A minimum set of activities described in irregularly shaped boxes and linked by arrows depicting logical dependencies.
	The boxes may be numbered for reference purposes and for reflecting levels without implying any sequence of activities.
Derivation	Set of elementary primary task conceptual models Tentative primary task model and the root definition derived from the tentative primary task model Test model
Quality	Criteria:

1   Do activities included in the model relate to words used in the root definition of the test model?

2   Does the description of an activity begin with a verb in the imperative?

3   Are monitor and control activities included?

4   Are the activities described at the same level of detail?

5   Do the activities and their logical dependencies form a coherent set?

6   Have activities to resolve conflicts been included?

External dependencies	Availability of people representing the cross-section of views expressed in the set of elementary primary task models to participate in the process.

References		
	Consensus primary task model building	Section 4.4.1
	Information activity tabulation	Section 4.4.2
	Maltese cross development	Section 4.5.1

An example model is given in Figure D2.

Annex D
SSM product descriptions
Consensus primary task model

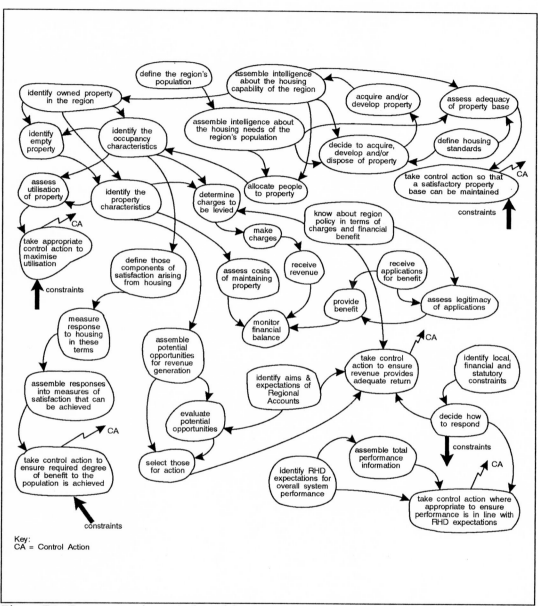

Figure D2: Consensus primary task model

D.3 Information activity table

Purpose	To record information categories which would be required as input to and output from CPTM activities and, where possible, measures of performance for those activities.
Composition	A column for each activity and three rows: inputs, outputs, and measures of performance. The inputs may be marked as internal (I) or external (E) according to whether they come from activities within the boundary of interest or from outside it.
Derivation	CPTM Discussions with potential users and potential providers of information.
Quality	Criteria:

    1 Does the table contain the minimum information categories needed to support activities within the boundary of interest?

    2 Is like information combined into one category?

    3 Is different information represented by separate categories?

    4 Can the measures of performance be used to judge how well any comparable existing activities are performed?

External dependencies	Availability of potential users and potential providers of information.

References		
	Information activity tabulation	Section 4.4.2
	Maltese cross development	Section 4.5.1

An example is given in Table D1.

Annex D
SSM product descriptions
Information activity table

Activity	Assess Costs of Maintaining Property	Allocate People to Property	Determine Charges to be Levied	Make Charges	Receive Revenue	Receive Application for Benefit	Assess Legitimacy of Claim	Provide Benefit	Monitor Balance
Inputs	Property List Maintenance Costs Region Boundary	Housing Application Empty Property Offer Acceptance Landlord Details Region Boundary Occupancy Priority Criteria Property Characteristics	Regional Policy Property Characteristics Occupancy Owner/ Occupier List Housing Benefit Claims	Occupancy Rent Service Charge	Bills Amounts Received	Benefit Application and Personal Details	Regional Policy Benefit Application Occupancy Debtors	Benefit Claim Personal Details Landlord Details	Revenue and Debtors Benefit Payments and Creditors Maintenance Costs
Outputs	Maintenance Costs	Allocations Occupancy Housing Applications Homeless Reports Allocation Offer	Rent Service Charge Rent Weighting	Bills	Revenue and Debtors	Benefit Application	Benefit Claim Regional Policy	Benefit Payments and Creditors	Balance Report
Measures of Performance			Admin Costs Expenditure/ Income	Shortfall in Income Expectations	Size of Debtors List				

Table D1: Information activity table

D.4 Maltese cross

Purpose	To allow comparison between information flows that would be required to support proposed system activities and information flows provided by existing information processing procedures.
Composition	A four-part matrix, the upper half containing activities and the lower half containing existing information processing procedures. The west axis represents inputs required to support the activities. The east axis is a mirror image of the west axis and represents outputs.
	A cross in either of the two western quadrants indicates a requirement for an information category. A cross in either of the eastern quadrants indicates the provision of an information category.
	Inputs which come from external sources are indicated by E instead of a cross.
	The southern quadrants and axis may be blank in a green field situation.
Derivation	CPTM Discussions with current users and current providers of information Organisation map Information activity table
Quality	Criteria: 1 Does the matrix represent the current state of the existing information processing procedures' network?
External dependencies	Availability of current users and current providers of information.
References	Maltese cross development Section 4.5.1 Recommendations formulation Section 4.5.1
	An example is given in Figure D3.

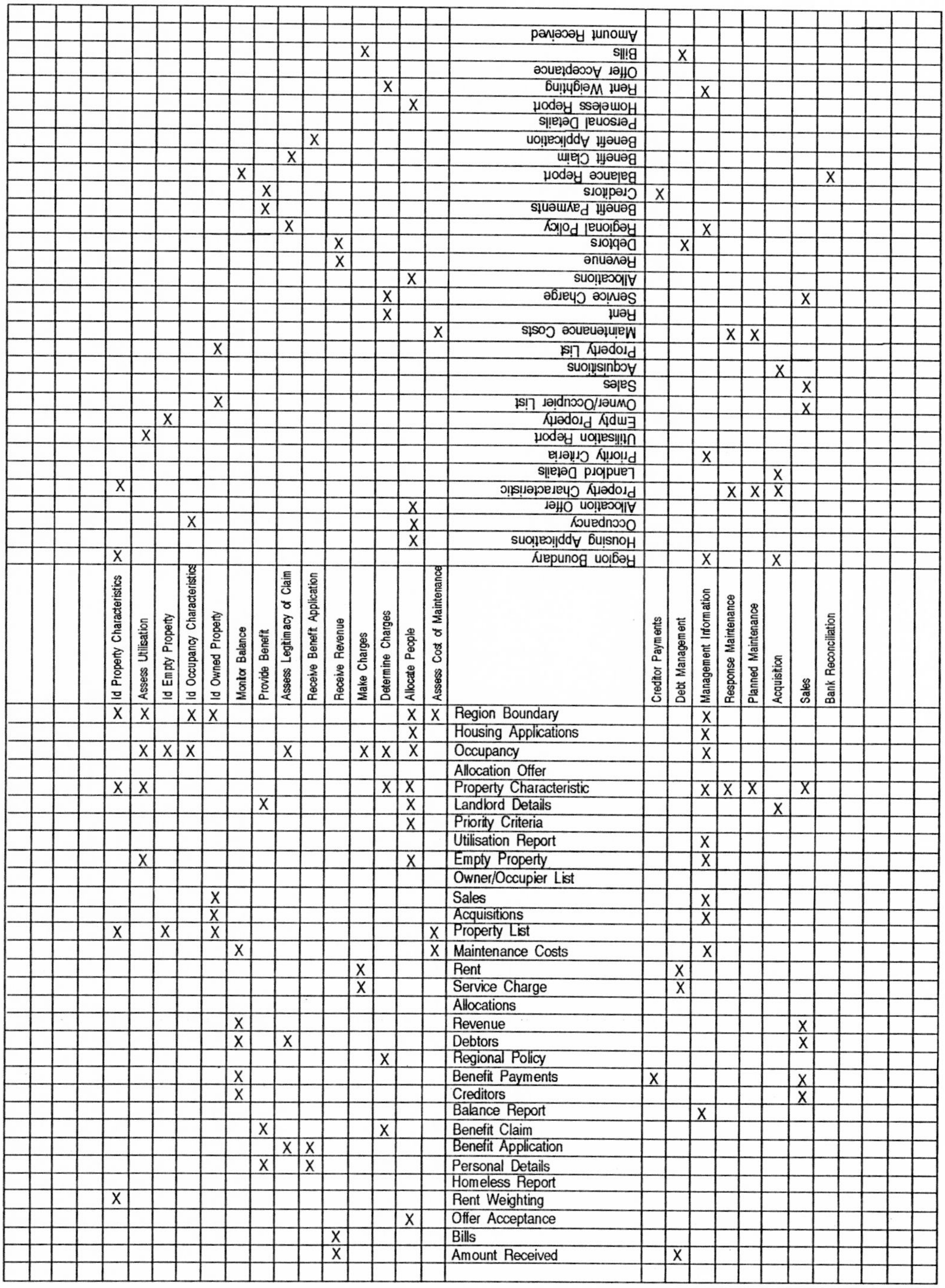

Figure D3: Maltese cross

The following transcribes the Maltese cross matrix. Because of its cross (quadrant) structure, it is presented here as two tables sharing the central list of entities: the left arm maps entities against processes, and the right arm maps entities against products/functions.

Entities × Processes (left arm)

Entity	Id Property Characteristics	Assess Utilisation	Id Empty Property	Id Occupancy Characteristics	Id Owned Property	Monitor Balance	Provide Benefit	Assess Legitimacy of Claim	Receive Benefit Application	Receive Revenue	Make Charges	Determine Charges	Allocate People	Assess Cost of Maintenance
Region Boundary	X	X											X	X
Housing Applications														
Occupancy			X	X	X				X			X	X	X
Allocation Offer														
Property Characteristic	X	X										X	X	X
Landlord Details								X						X
Priority Criteria														X
Utilisation Report														
Empty Property		X												X
Owner/Occupier List														
Sales						X								
Acquisitions						X								
Property List	X			X	X									X
Maintenance Costs						X								X
Rent											X			
Service Charge											X			
Allocations														
Revenue						X								
Debtors						X		X						
Regional Policy												X		
Benefit Payments						X								
Creditors						X								
Balance Report														
Benefit Claim							X		X					
Benefit Application								X	X					
Personal Details							X		X					
Homeless Report														
Rent Weighting	X													
Offer Acceptance													X	
Bills											X			
Amount Received										X				

Entities × Products (right arm)

Entity	Creditor Payments	Debt Management	Management Information	Response Maintenance	Planned Maintenance	Acquisition	Sales	Bank Reconciliation
Region Boundary			X					
Housing Applications			X					
Occupancy			X					
Allocation Offer								
Property Characteristic			X	X	X	X		
Landlord Details				X				
Priority Criteria			X					
Utilisation Report			X					
Empty Property			X					
Owner/Occupier List								
Sales						X		
Acquisitions						X		
Property List								
Maintenance Costs			X					
Rent		X						
Service Charge		X						
Allocations								
Revenue							X	
Debtors							X	
Regional Policy								
Benefit Payments	X						X	
Creditors							X	
Balance Report		X						
Benefit Claim								
Benefit Application								
Personal Details								
Homeless Report								
Rent Weighting								
Offer Acceptance								
Bills								
Amount Received		X						

Figure D3: Maltese cross

107

D.5   Organisation mapping

Purpose	To identify possible anomalies in an organisation's existing structure by comparing actual allocation of responsibilities for activities in conceptual subsystems.
Composition	A base chart, ie a CPTM showing only second level activities, and two transparent overlays. The first overlay shows subsystem boundaries and the second notes current decision-taking authority for each activity.
Derivation	CPTM Discussions with current decision-takers
Quality	Criteria:

1   Are subsystem boundaries clearly defined?

2   Do the names given to sub-systems differ sufficiently from those of current organisational units in order to maintain a clear distinction between conceptual and physical groupings?

3   Are island activities, ie those whose current responsibility is different from that implied by subsystem boundaries, highlighted?

4   Are activities for which no current decision-taking authority exists highlighted?

External dependencies	Availability of current decision-takers for discussions.

References		
	Organisational mapping	Section 4.5.2
	Maltese cross development	Section 4.5.1

An example is given in Figure D4.

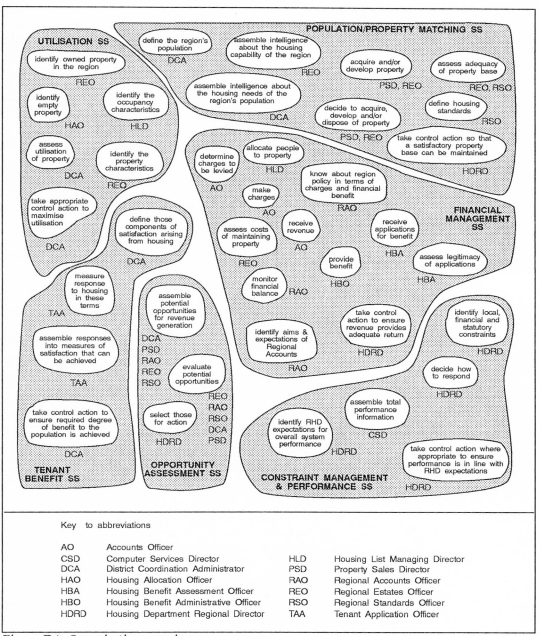

Figure D4: Organisation mapping

D.6 Rich picture

Purpose

To illustrate the structure and processes of an existing situation which may have perceived problems or which may be the subject for study and proposed change.

Its construction gives the analyst a deeper understanding of a business unit and the environment in which it operates. The rich picture may be used to communicate this understanding to other parties.

Provides an historical description of a situation.

Composition

The picture is composed of symbols, chosen by the analyst, which represent, for example, people and objects involved in the situation and arrows to show relationships between them.

The meanings of the symbols may be defined in a key.

Derivation

Project Initiation Document
Discussions with interested parties
Management statements
Organisation charts
Other relevant background information

Quality

Criteria:

For a single picture:

1 Does the picture describe the business of the situation under review?

2 Does it present a comprehensive view of the situation without being cluttered with too much detail?

3 Is the boundary of the area of concern marked on the rich picture?

4 Are relationships, including conflicts, between its components described?

5 Are the roles of people involved indicated?

6   Are organisational issues noted?

7   Are external constraints shown?

8   Are supporting facts or figures suitably represented?

9   Are the expectations of controlling authorities documented?

10 Are symbols used consistently and their meanings described where necessary?

Where more than one rich picture is produced:

11 Do symbols common to more than one picture have the same meaning?

External dependencies   Management commitment to providing resources

References   Rich picture building   Section 4.2
                        Root definition formulation   Section 3.4

An example is given in Figure D5.

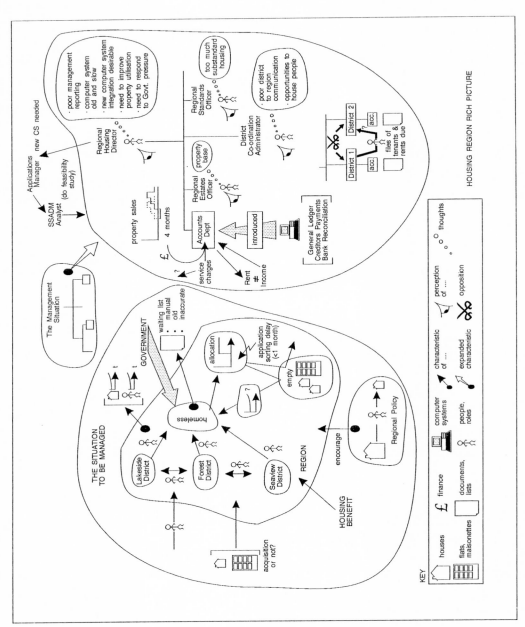

Figure D5: Rich picture

D.7   Root definition

Purpose

To describe what a system is, based on a particular belief in its purpose (see W below).

Composition

A concise description of a human activity system consisting of six elements which may be remembered by the mnemonic CATWOE:

C   Customer, the recipient of the transformation process

A   Actors or agents who would do the activities if the model were to map on to reality

T   The transformation process

W   Weltanschauung or World-view, the belief contained in the root definition

O   Owner, the wider system decision-taker with concern for the performance of the system

E   Environmental constraints, features of the real world that the definition needs to recognise but outside the control of the system's decision-taking process.

T is mandatory and W is usually implicit in the description rather than explicitly stated.

Derivation

Rich picture
Discussions with interested parties
CATWOE analysis

Quality

Criteria:

For a single root definition:

1   Is the definition well formulated in that it stands up to CATWOE analysis?

2   Does the definition contain only one transformation?

3   Is there 100% commitment to a single W?

4   Has the definition been agreed by someone who might subscribe to that point of view?

5   Does the definition contain only necessary words?

6   If the definition is for a subsystem, is it consistent with the definition for the higher-level system which owns it?

For a set of root definitions:

7   Are all main bodies of opinion represented?

8   Are conflicting or extreme views represented?

9   Have similar views been amalgamated into a single definition?

External dependencies   Interested parties are available for involvement in the validation exercise. Management commitment to providing resources.

References   Root definition formulation   Section 3.4
              Conceptual model building   Section 3.5

Example root definitions are given opposite.

**Example root
definitions**

Regional Housing
Director's view

The following root definitions represent the views of
key roles in the Regional Housing Directorate example.

"A Regional Housing Directorate owned and operated
system to provide housing for the population of the
region to the benefit of both the region and the people
within the constraints of the locality, finance and
relevant statutory regulations."

The CATWOE analysis for the above root definition is:

C the population of the Region

A the Regional Housing Directorate

T to provide housing for occupancy

W providing housing is beneficial to the region and to
the people

O the Regional Housing Directorate

E constraints of the locality, finance and relevant
statutory regulations

The District Coordination Administrator (DCA) would
have a similar view, but operating at district level. For
instance, an expansion of the activity "assess the degree
to which benefit is achieved" in the conceptual model
derived from the above root definition might be:

"A District Coordination Administrator owned system
to assess benefit in terms of degree of satisfaction to the
tenants and revenue generating opportunities for the
directorate."

Regional Estates
Officer's view

"A Regional Housing Directorate owned system to
maximise the utilisation of its owned property in order
to obtain a satisfactory return on its investment while
recognising local, financial, and statutory constraints
and the regional housing policy."

A subsystem model dealing with return on investment could be developed from the root definition:

"A Regional Accounts owned system which converts the occupancy/non-occupancy of the region's property into the revenue necessary to provide an adequate return on investment while recognising statutory constraints and the Region's policy with respect to finance."

Regional Standards Officer's view

"A Regional Housing Directorate owned system to maintain and develop its property base so that adequate standards of housing can be achieved in relation to the accommodation needs of the region while recognising local, financial and statutory constraints."

Regional Accounts Officer's view

One of several possible root definitions might have been: "A Regional Housing Directorate owned system to respond to government pressure by replacing existing rates procedures by a new Community Charge in order to finance its regional services."

Other viewpoints

Other viewpoints from which root definitions could be constructed include:

Regional Accounts Officer:

> ... system to collect payments due from property occupiers for rent and services...

Property Sales Director:

> ... system to sell under-utilised property owned by the Regional Housing Directorate...

Property Sales Director:

> ... system to support legislated right-to-buy of tenants of publicly-owned housing.

Bibliography

Information Systems Guides   The Information Systems Guides, published by CCTA, are available from John Wiley & Sons Ltd, Baffins Lane, Chichester PO19 1UD.

The following guides are referenced in this publication:

CCTA IS Guides A2: Strategic Planning for Information Systems
ISBN: 0 471 92526 8

CCTA IS Guides B2: Feasibility Study
ISBN: 0 471 92527 6

Information Systems Engineering Library   The Information Systems Engineering Library volumes, published by CCTA, are available from HMSO Publications Centre, PO Box 276, London SW8 5DT.

The following volume is referenced in this publication:

SSADM in an IS Strategy Environment
ISBN: 0 11 330579 6

SSADM documentation   The SSADM Version 4 Reference Manual is published by NCC/Blackwell and is available from The Publications Manager, National Computer Centre Ltd, Oxford Road, Manchester M1 7ED.
ISBN: 1 85554 004 5.

PRINCE documentation   PRINCE: Structured Project Management is published by NCC/Blackwell and is available from The Publications Manager, National Computer Centre Ltd, Oxford Road, Manchester M1 7ED.
ISBN: 1 85554 012 6.

Glossary

activity

A neutral term for the carrying out of an act, contrasting with action and behaviour. The word is used in 'human activity system' to emphasise that such systems are not descriptions of observed real-world action.

actor

In CATWOE, a person who carries out one or more of the activities in the system.

Business System Options (BSO)

Used in SSADM to define the functionality needs and the boundary for a system, with reference to the business needs.

CATWOE

A mnemonic of the six characteristics that may be included in a well-formulated root definition:

- Customer
- Actor
- Transformation Process
- Weltanschauung (or World-view)
- Owner (of the problem situation or system)
- Environmental Constraints.

conceptual model

A systemic account of a human activity system built on the basis of that system's root definition, usually in the form of a structured set of verbs in the imperative mood. Such models should contain the minimum necessary activities for the system to be the one named in the root definition. Only activities that could be directly carried out should be included.

consensus primary task model (CPTM)

A conceptual model, derived from other conceptual models representing different Weltanschauungen (world-views), by a process of debate with the relevant population of individuals leading to an accommodation of their Weltanschauungen.

customer

In CATWOE, the beneficiary or victim of the system's activity.

Data Flow Diagram (DFD)	An SSADM product which shows how services are organised and processing is undertaken. It should be a simple diagram that is readily understood, so that it can act as a an effective means of communication between analysts and users.
Data Flow Model (DFM)	A set of Data Flow Diagrams and their associated documentation. The diagrams form a hierarchy with the Data Flow Diagram Level 1 showing the scope of the system and the lower levels expanding the detail as appropriate. Additional documentation provides a description of the processes, input/output data flows and external entities.
environmental constraints	In CATWOE, impositions which the system takes as given.
human activity system (HAS)	A notional system which expresses some purposeful human activity, activity which could in principle be found in the real world. Such systems are notional in the sense that they are not descriptions of actual real-world action but are intellectual constructs; they are ideal types for use in a debate about possible changes which might be introduced into a real-world problem situation.
information	This is taken to be data plus the meaning ascribed to it.
Logical Data Model (LDM)	An SSADM product which provides an accurate model of the information requirements of all or part of an organisation. It consists of a Logical Data Structure and associated descriptions of entities and relationships.
Logical Data Structure (LDS)	A diagrammatic representation of the information needs of an organisation in the form of entities and the important business relationships between them.
logicalisation	SSADM technique used in data flow modelling in which data-stores are rationalised, bottom-level processes are rationalised and regrouped, and the Logical DFD is checked for consistency and completeness.

Maltese cross A display device in the form of a 4-part matrix which enables a comparison to be made between information requirements derived from a conceptual model, and information provision derived from the actual data processing present in the situation.

model An intellectual construct, descriptive of an entity in which at least one observer has an interest. The observer may wish to relate his model and, if appropriate, its mechanisms, to observables in the real world. When this is done it frequently leads, understandably but not accurately, to descriptions of the world couched in terms of models, as if the world were identical with models of it.

modelling language A class, or set of classes of elements used to construct models. For example, the modelling language suitable for making models of human activity systems is: all the verbs in the natural language; an indicator of logical dependency; indicators of flows, concrete or abstract.

owner In CATWOE, the person or persons who could modify or demolish the system.

problem situation A connected group of real world-events and ideas which at least one person perceives as problematic; for him, other possibilities concerning the situation are worth investigating.

Project Initiation Document (PID) A product approved by the project board. It defines the terms of reference and objectives for the project. It is used to identify business requirements, as well as organisational and general information needs, security aspects and an initial project plan.

relational data analysis (RDA) A technique used in SSADM for deriving data structures which have the least redundant data and the most flexibility.

rich picture The expression of a problem situation compiled by an investigator, often by examining elements of structure, elements of processes and the relationship between these elements.

root definition	A concise, tightly-constructed description of a human activity system which states what the system is; what it does is then elaborated in a conceptual model which is built on the basis of the definition. Every element in the definition must be reflected in the model derived from it.
root definition, issue-based	A root definition describing a notional system chosen for its relevance to what the investigator and/or the people in the problem situation perceive as a matter of contention.
root definition, primary task	A root definition of a system which carries out some major task manifest in the real world.
subsystem	Equivalent to system, but contained in some larger system.
system	A model of a whole entity; when applied to human activity, the model is characterised fundamentally in terms of hierarchical structure, emergent properties, communication and control. An observer may choose to relate this model to real-world activity. When applied to natural or man-made entities, the crucial characteristic is the emergent properties of the whole.
systematic	Constituted as a set of well-defined components, with well-defined relationships between them, that can be dealt with in an ordered sequence of tasks.
systemic	To be regarded as a whole system, so that behaviour or change is behaviour or change of the whole, rather than individual parts of the system.
Technical System Options (TSO)	A set of options developed in SSADM so that the system development direction can be chosen. Each option documents the functions to be incorporated and details implementation requirements.
transformation process	In CATWOE, the core transformation process of a human activity system, which can be expressed as the conversion of some input into some output.

Weltanschauung (W)	In CATWOE, the unquestioned image or model of the world that makes a particular human activity system, with its transformation process, a meaningful one to consider.
Weltanschauungen (Ws)	Plural of Weltanschauung.
wider system	Equivalent to system but containing it.

Index

Printed in the United Kingdom for HMSO
Dd297185 10/93 C7 531/3 12521